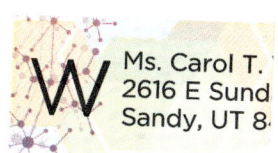

Ms. Carol T.
2616 E Sund
Sandy, UT 8

MW01580094

May the Spirit of the Aurora light up your life!

Jimmy Tohill

The Spirit of Alaska
AURORA EDITION

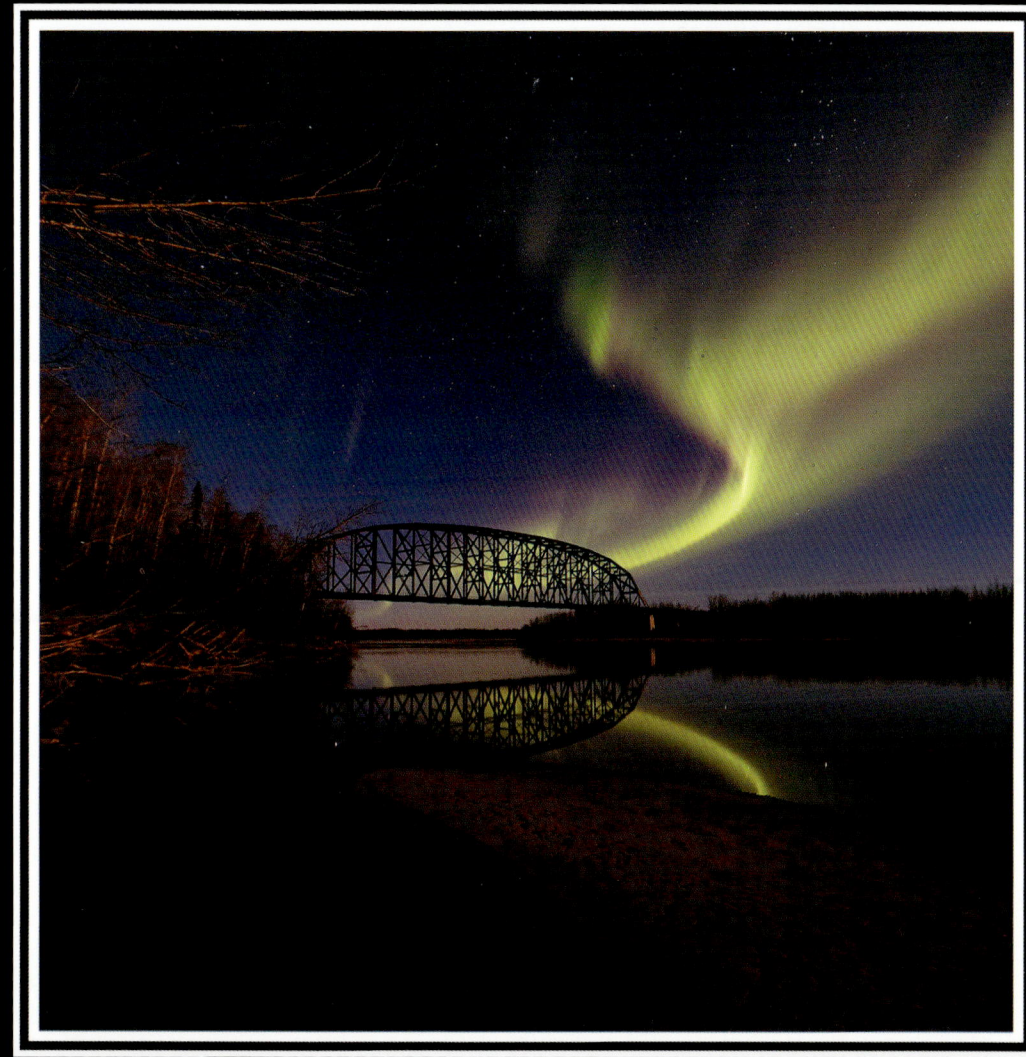

by Jimmy Tohill

The Spirit of Alaska ~ Aurora Edition

Copyright © 2018 by Jimmy Tohill. All rights reserved. This book may not be reproduced in whole or in part without the written consent of the publisher.

Library of Congress Control Number: 2018944319

ISBN: 9781578336999

First Printing: June, 2018

Photography and poetry - Jimmy Tohill
Design and layout - Jimmy Tohill
Final file preparation - Crystal Burrell / Todd Communications

Printed by Everbest Printing Investment., Ltd., Guangzhou, China
through **Alaska Print Brokers**, Anchorage, Alaska

Published in Healy, Alaska by Jimmy Tohill / Old Sourdough Studio - Denali

For additional copies contact :
Jimmy and Vicki Tohill / Old Sourdough Studio
P.O. Box 455 Healy, Ak 99743
907-683-1011
oss@mtaonline.net
www.oldsourdoughstudio.com
www.thespiritofalaska.com

or stop by **Old Sourdough Studio**
at the McKinley Chalet Resort - Mile 239 Parks Hwy., Denali, AK

Cover photo: a fast moving, brilliant aurora along with a quarter moon light up Mt. Healy and silhouette a bronze caribou sculpture at the Denali Princess Wilderness Lodge in the Nenana Canyon just north of the entrance to Denali National Park ~ March 25, 1:15 am.

The Spirit of Alaska ~ Aurora Edition

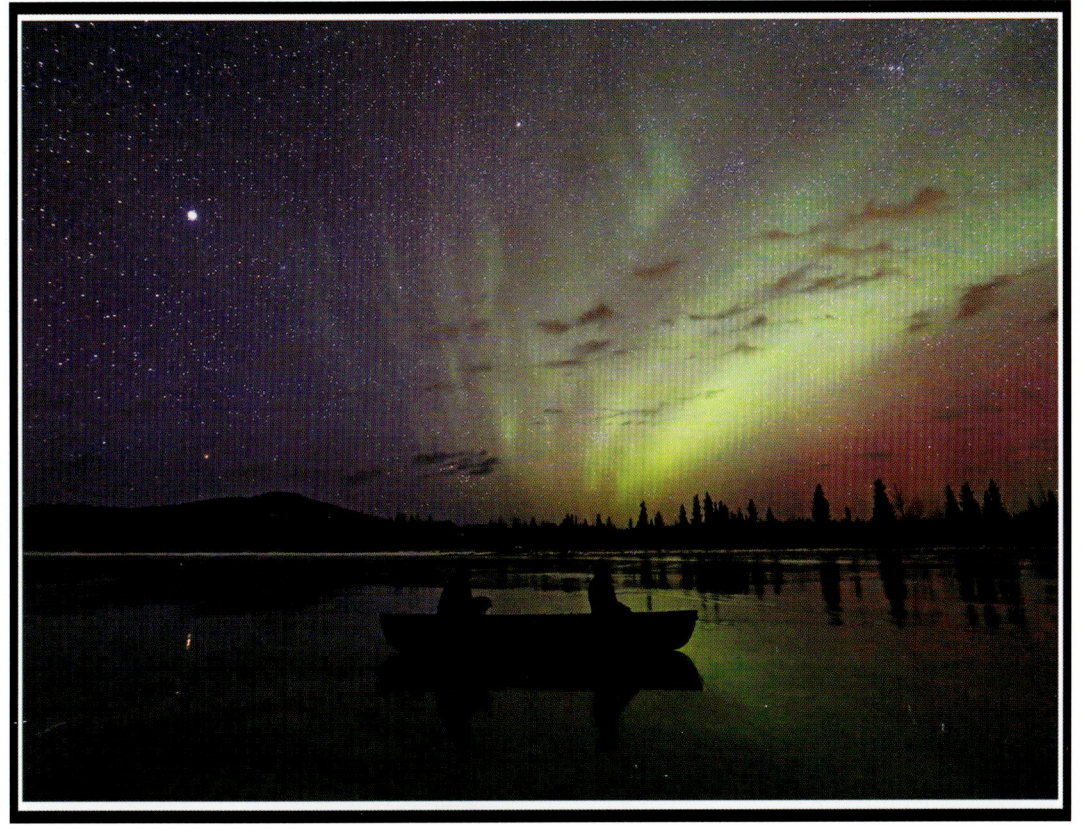

Table of Contents

Explanations and Observations 5, 6
The Spirit of Alaska ~ Aurora Edition 11
Dance of the Lights 21, 22
Cold and Dark 29, 30
An Awakening of Light 43
Precious Moments 53
Colors Swirling in the Sky 61, 62
The Beauty of No Indoor Plumbing. 81

About the Photographer / Poet 93
Index (description of photos) 94, 95, 96

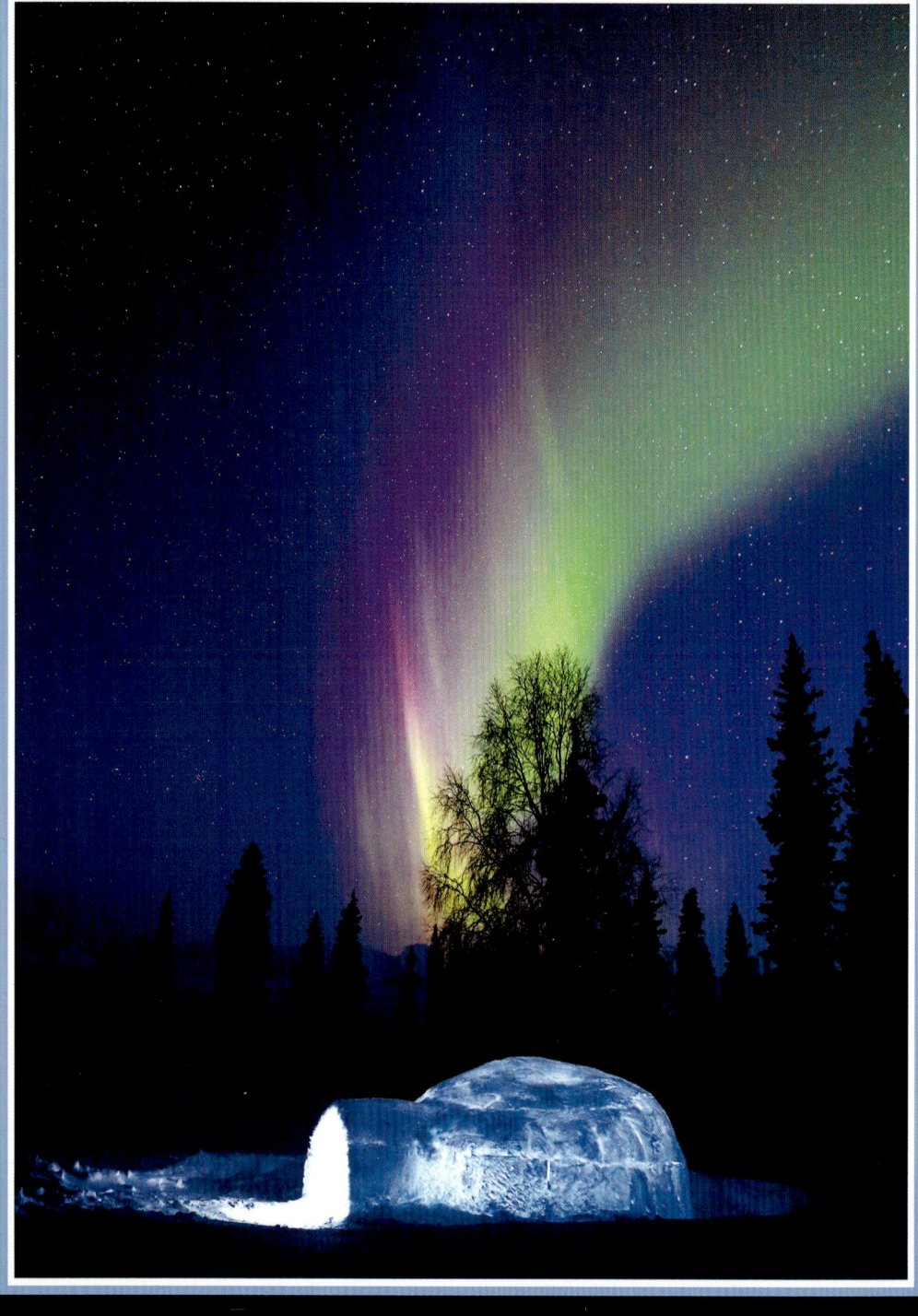

Explanations and Observations

To witness the northern lights during an active auroral storm is breathtaking to say the least. But let it be known that the aurora is a fickle phenomenon in the sense that you just never know what you're going to see. An auroral display can vary from a static greenish, white arc low on the horizon to a dazzling, wildly pulsating array of colors straight overhead that change shape and intensity so fast it is hard to take it all in. Often times the aurora will gradually evolve from the static greenish, white arc to the wildly pulsating, intense colors and back to the low angle arc several times in the course of a night. When activity is high, the aurora displays can last all night with peak and lull intensity. The peak intensity displays generally tend to last around 30 minutes and the lulls in between can be up to 2 hours. Sometimes they only come out and last for 15 or 20 minutes and other times during forecasted high activity they do not happen at all. So I have found that in order to get the best chance of viewing the aurora and experiencing its diversity of displays it helps to be devoted and ready to be out all night, or at least for 3 or 4 hours, when the aurora forecast is predicted to be active and the sky is clear. Even though the best time to see the aurora is between 10 pm and 2 am I have seen dazzling displays right up until the sun comes up to fade them out at 5:00 - 6:30 am in March and early April and I have seen amazing displays right after it got dark around 5 pm in January. So when it's dark and clear keep your eyes on the sky.

Although I have experienced amazing displays of the aurora borealis every month there is darkness, which is mid August through late April in interior Alaska, I tend to have better luck from December through April with March and April standing out as my most successful months of seeing and photographing stunning displays. Don't get me wrong - there are certainly lots of periods of auroral activity culminating in fantastic displays in the fall, it's just that the fall tends to be more cloudy than the winter and spring, and cloudy skies are not what you want for seeing the aurora. However, it does vary from year to year and there are good weather windows in every season.

I have heard many people say to try and avoid a full or near full moon. This is certainly the case if the aurora is not very intense, but, if there is a highly active auroral storm creating strong displays, the full moon will not be a negative issue; in fact, it can actually enhance photos by lighting up landmarks and foregrounds, and a full moon sure makes it easier to see what you are doing. The photo on the cover of this book was taken while the moon

Explanations and Observations

was quite bright and I have many photos throughout the book that were taken during a full moon.

One thing that really helps with your chances of seeing the aurora is being under, or nearly under, the auroral oval. The auroral oval is a huge ring above the Earth's geomagnetic poles that, in the north, is generally centered at about the arctic circle and is usually a couple hundred miles wide. It is ever changing due to solar winds caused from activity on the sun. These solar winds carry charged sub atomic particles through space that become attracted into Earth's atmosphere along the auroral oval. The more activity on the sun, the more charged particles are carried by solar winds, the larger the auroral oval gets and the more intense the aurora can become.

Different colors of the aurora come from charged particles colliding mainly with high and low level oxygen and nitrogen molecules exciting them into glowing. It is similar to a neon sign where a charged current is travelling through a gas filled tube exciting the gas atoms and making them glow. In the aurora's case, when these charged particles from the sun collide with oxygen at about 60 miles up it gives off the familiar yellow-green color. When colliding with oxygen at higher altitudes, about 150 - 200 miles, it gives the all red auroras. Collisions with ionic nitrogen produces the blue light and neutral nitrogen gives off the red-purple and the pinkish rippled edges. I have noticed that if auroral displays are active during a setting or rising sun there can be some noticeable color variations in the aurora's appearance.

I have tried to compile a nice variety of what auroral displays can offer through my photographs included in this book. Some of the images may seem a little redundant, but this is an attempt to show the ever, and sometimes very quickly, changing aspects of the aurora. Although some of these photogragh are quite amazing and very intriguing to look at, an active auroral display is truly an astonishing natural phenomenon that needs to be experienced first hand in order to really be blown away. To stand beneath a large night sky filled with rapidly curtaining waves of color that stretch overhead and turn into brilliantly colored pulsating rays that change shape and intensity faster than you can blink is truly an amazing experience.

Please enjoy these images, thoughts and insights I have gathered out under the sweet northern sky. ~ Jimmy

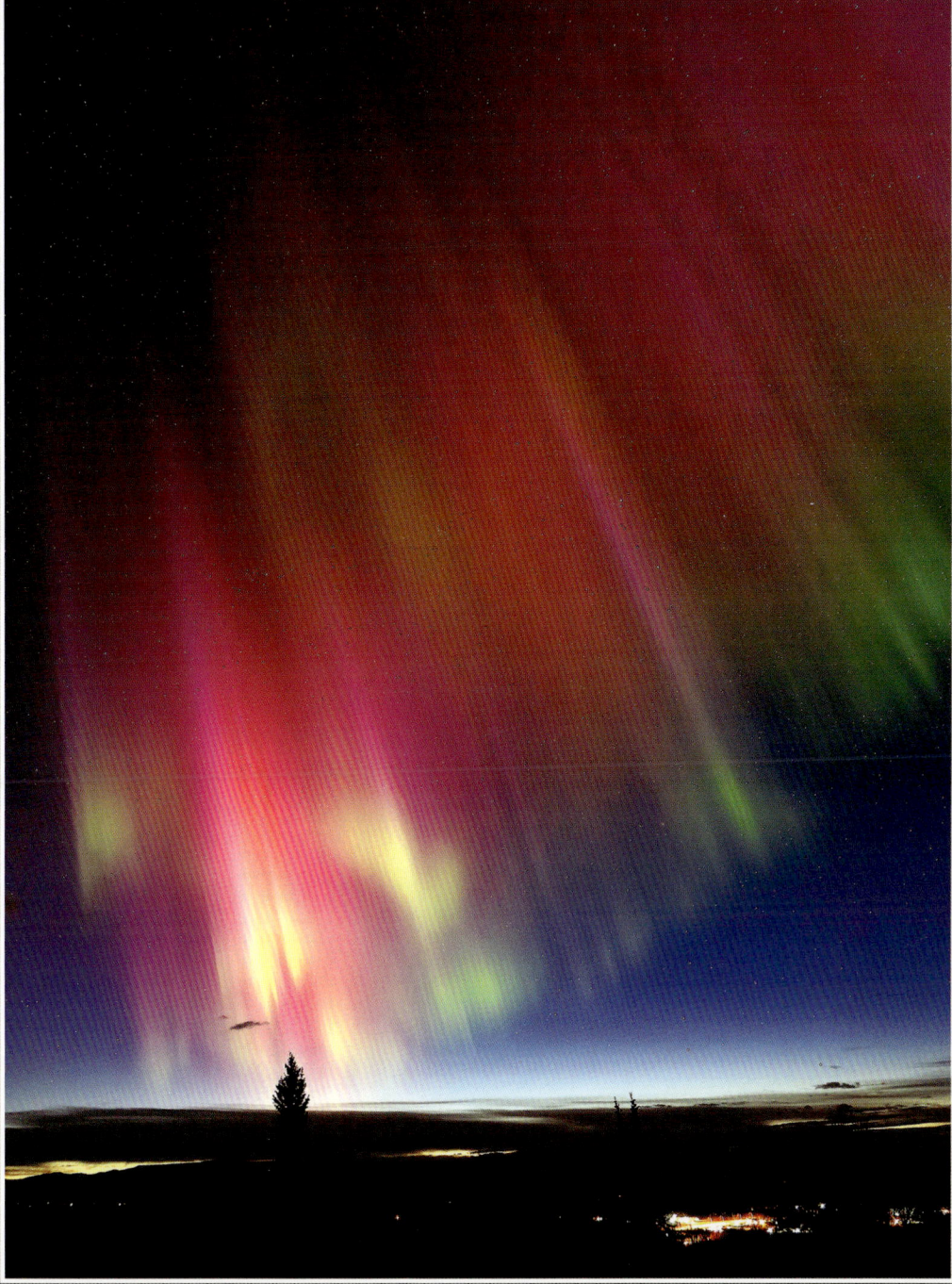

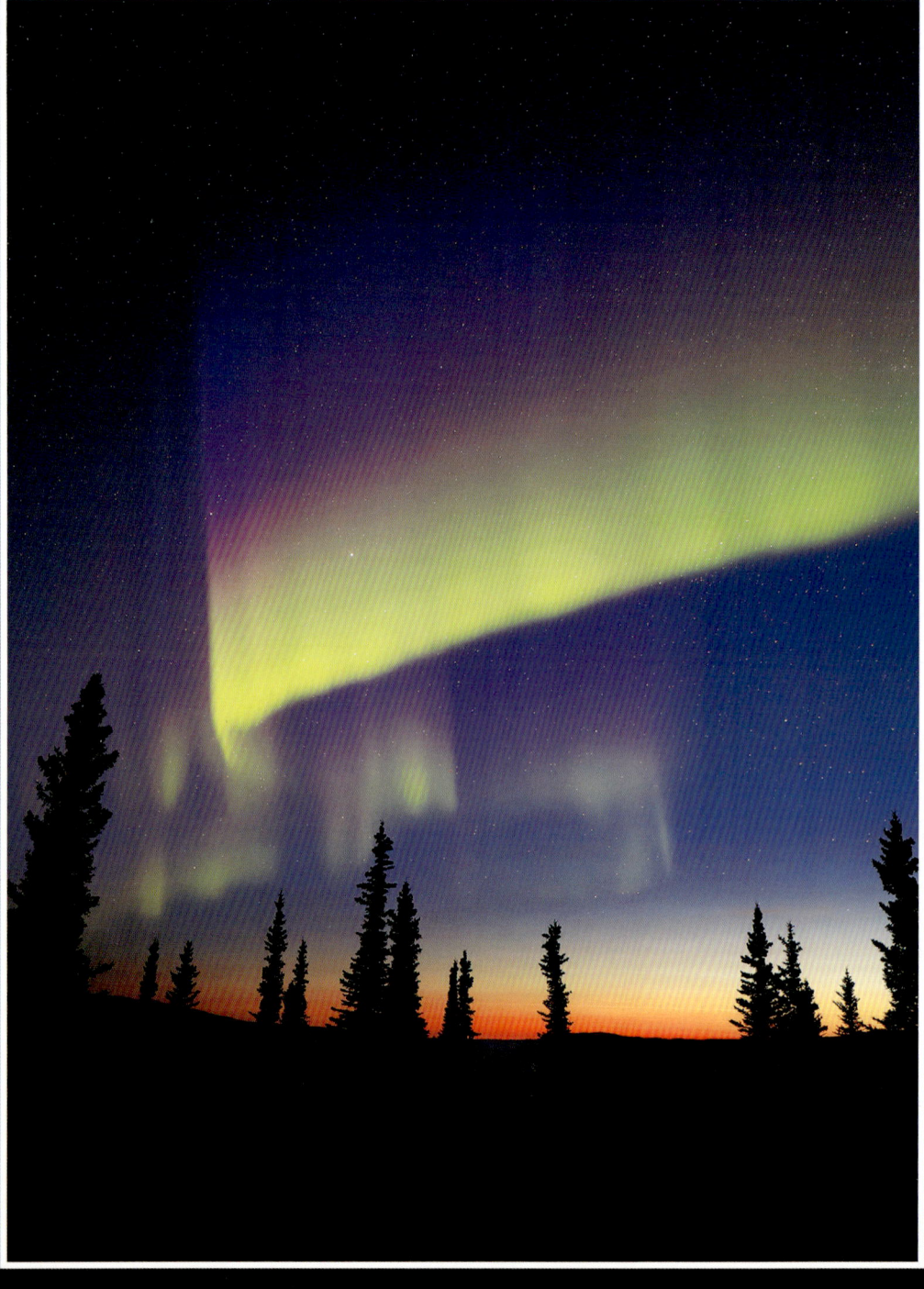

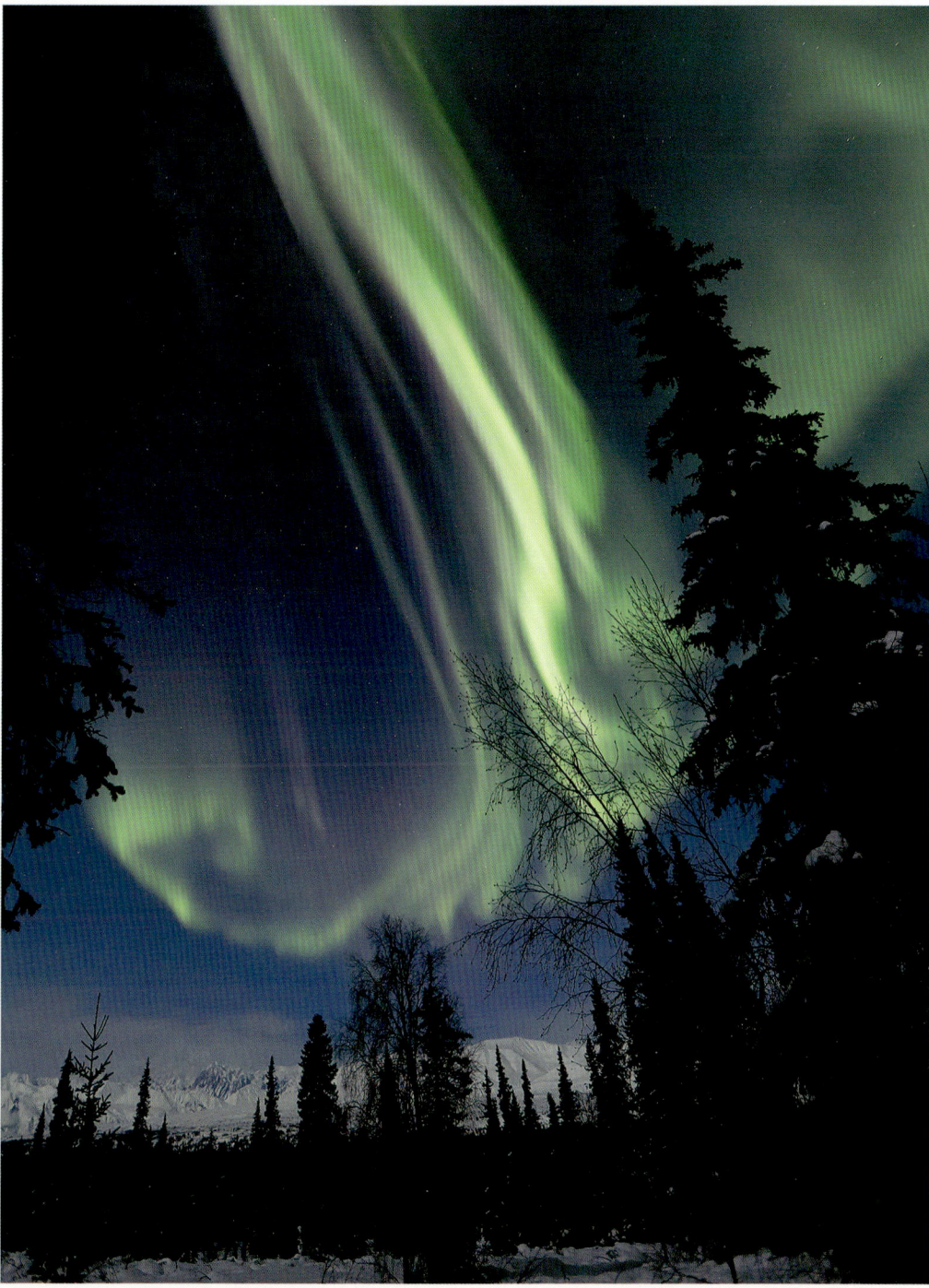

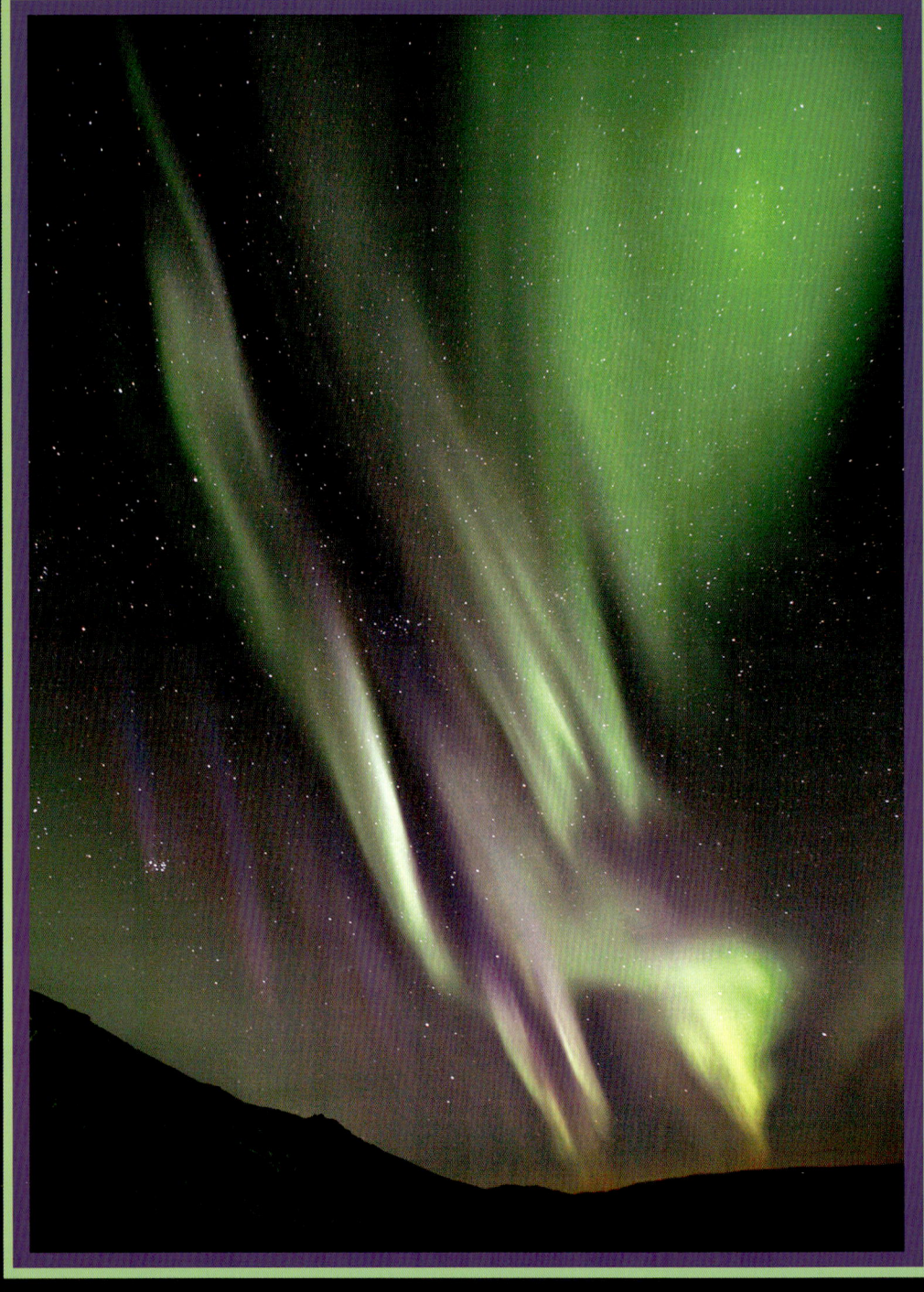

The Spirit of Alaska ~ Aurora Edition

The peaks are covered with snow and the wind begins to blow
  as the season with darkness returns to the land.
Autumn comes in fairly fast and just doesn't seem to last
  but it is the beginning of something quite grand.

As the dark night skies appear each and every passing year
  there is a phenomenon that will come and will go.
It is the aurora borealis which is grander than any palace
  and when active puts on an extravagant light show.

When the aurora is strong you just can't go wrong
  by witnessing the incredible sights.
The sights are unique and you can feel the mystique
  of the enchantment of the northern lights.

The Spirit of Alaska is there with the aurora glowing in the air
  and it brings about a true awareness of wonder.
With colors swirling in the sky, an exploding corona catches your eye,
  you stand in awe at the sky you are under.

From mid August to April's end the dark night sky is your friend
  if it is the aurora that you would like to see.
When the night sky is clear and the northern lights do appear
  you will gaze up at the heavens with glee.

There is certainly a strong sense when the aurora turns intense
  and the sky fills with pulsating colorful rays.
There is a feeling of real peace that just will not cease
  while experiencing these cosmic displays.

You will find a presence of being with what you are seeing
  while watching this marvel unfold.
Knowing that we are part of the universe's art
  is something to deeply behold.

Viewing the northern lights on cold starry nights,
  there's not a whole lot that can really compare.
It will make your head spin as you try and take it all in;
  this is just a part of what the Spirit of Alaska can share.

The Spirit of Alaska is awake and make no mistake
  it is steady and ready to shine.
The spirit of the aurora is alive and in your heart it can thrive
  because it is part of the great design.

May the spirit of the aurora shine on you!

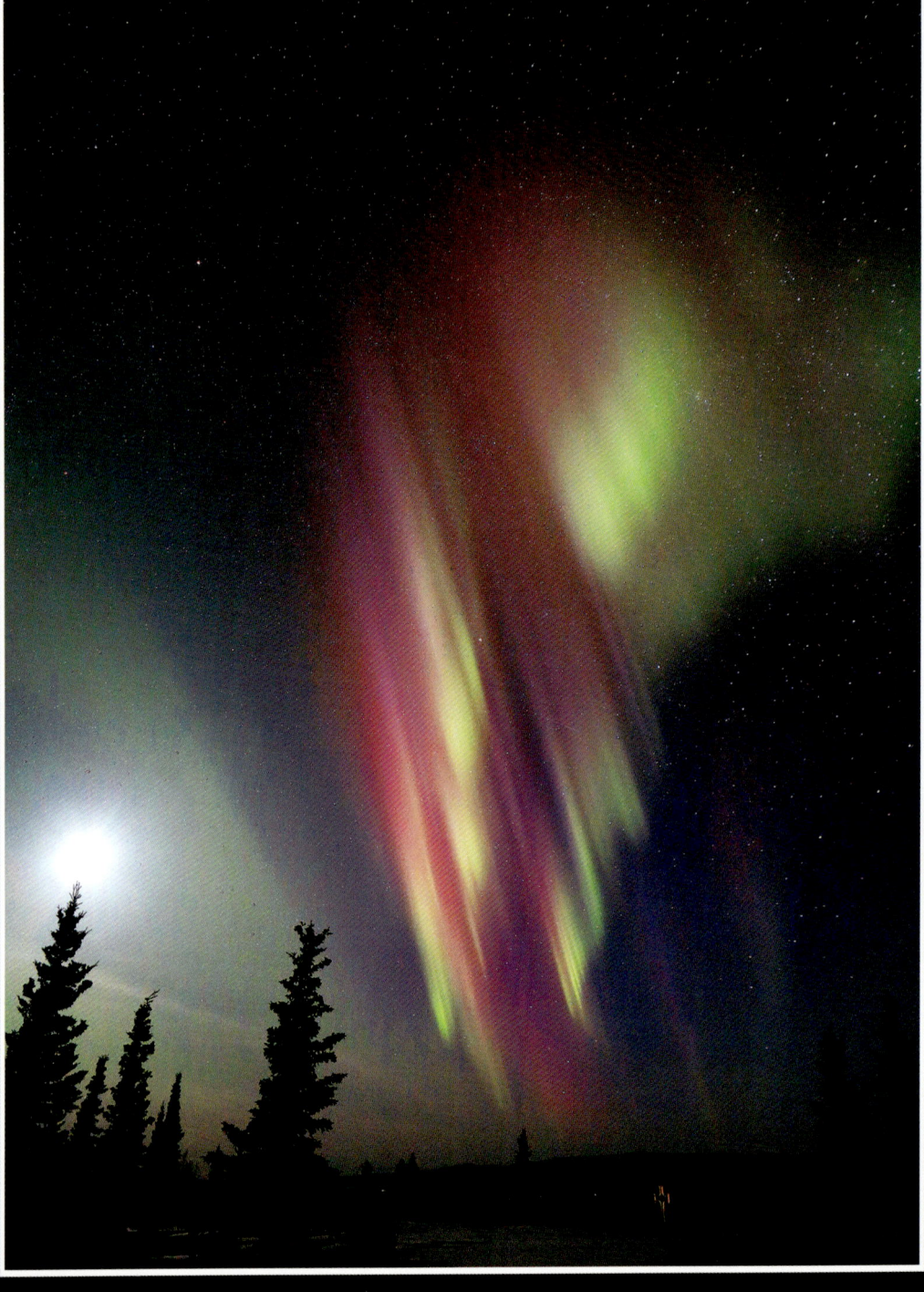

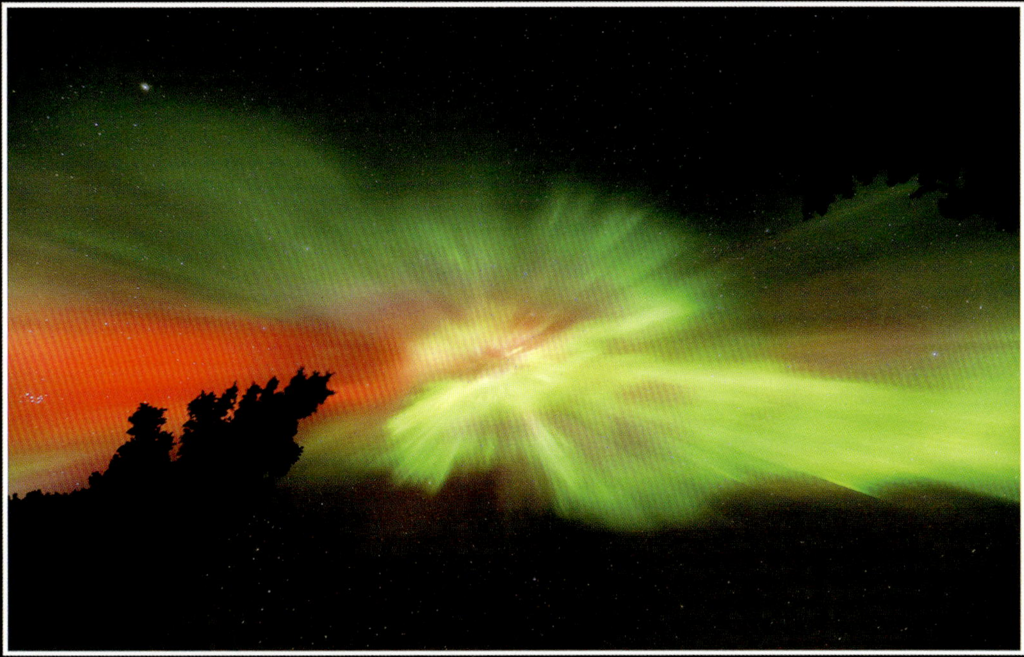

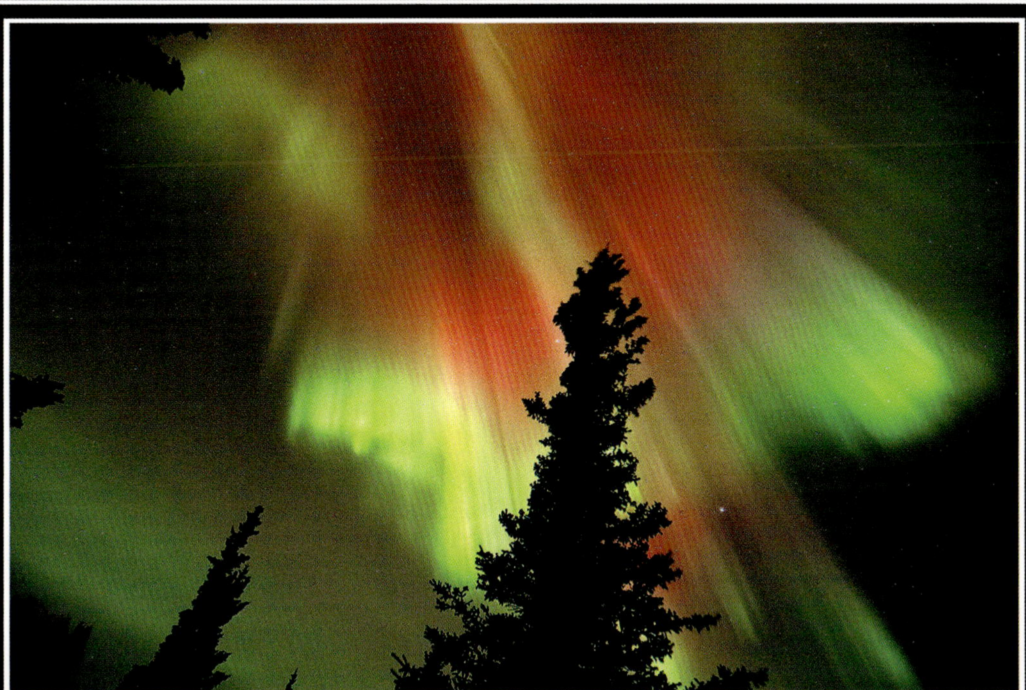

13

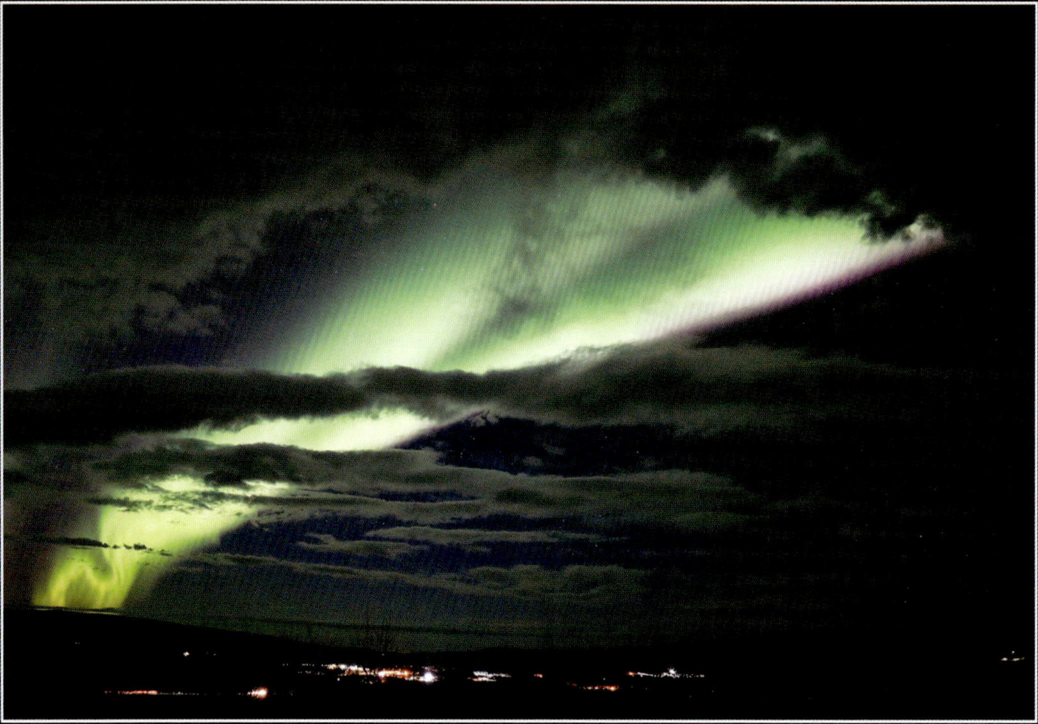

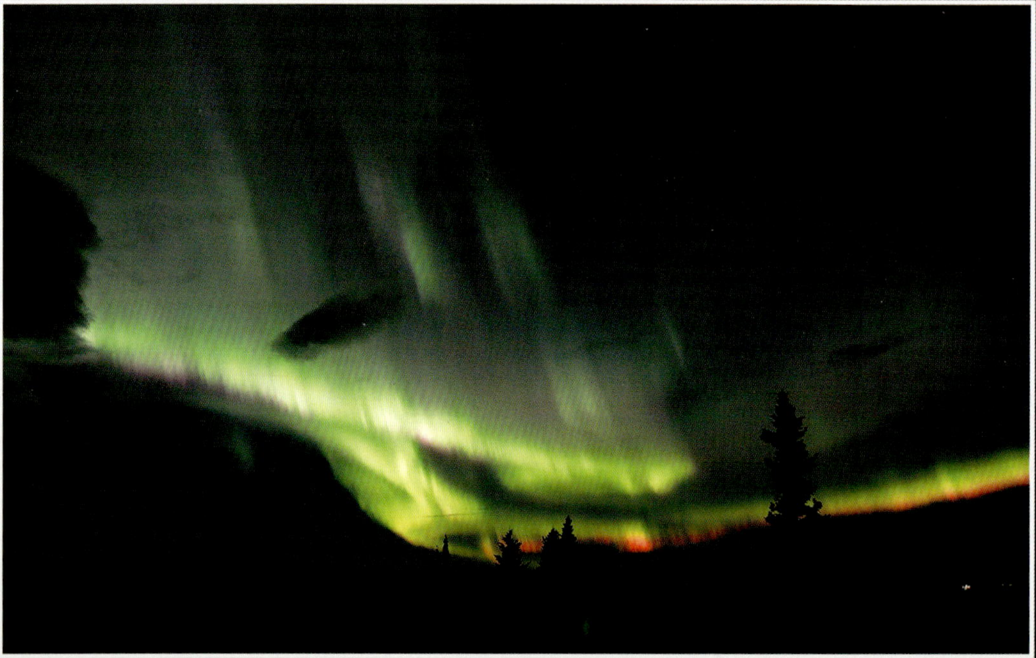

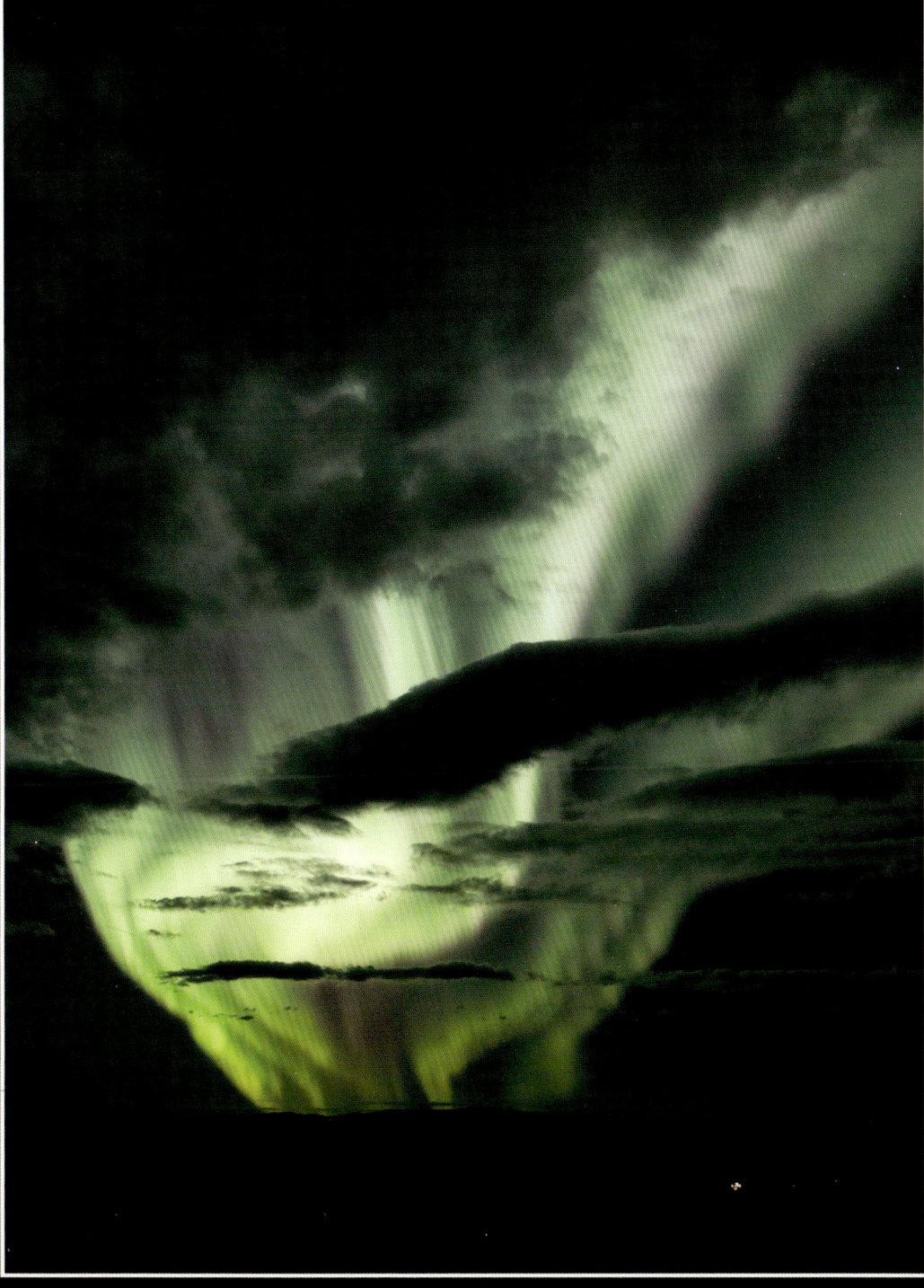

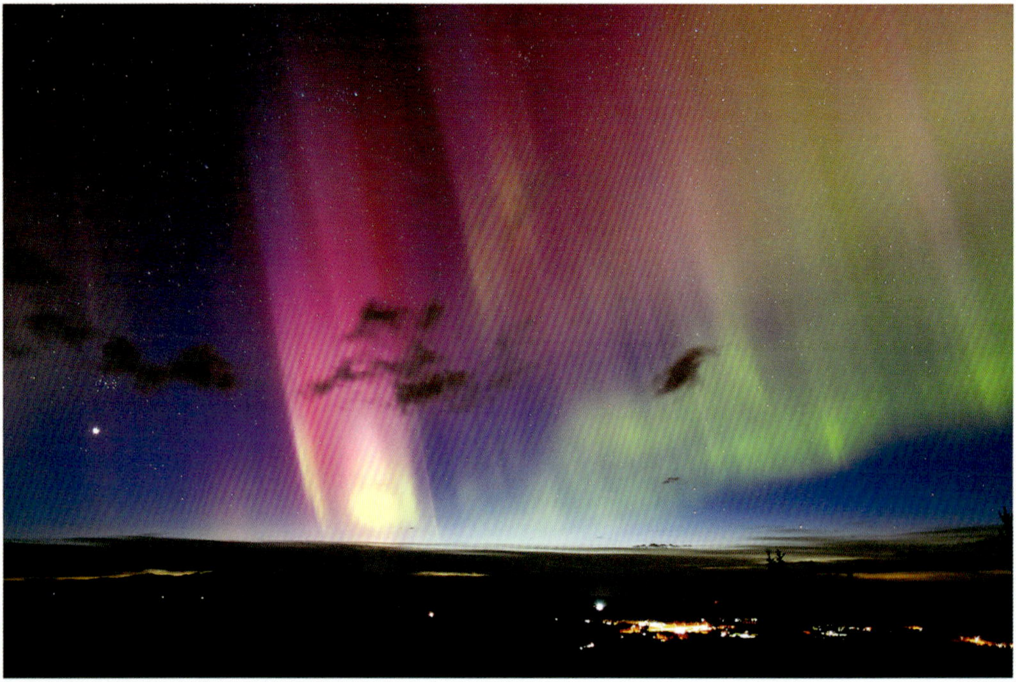

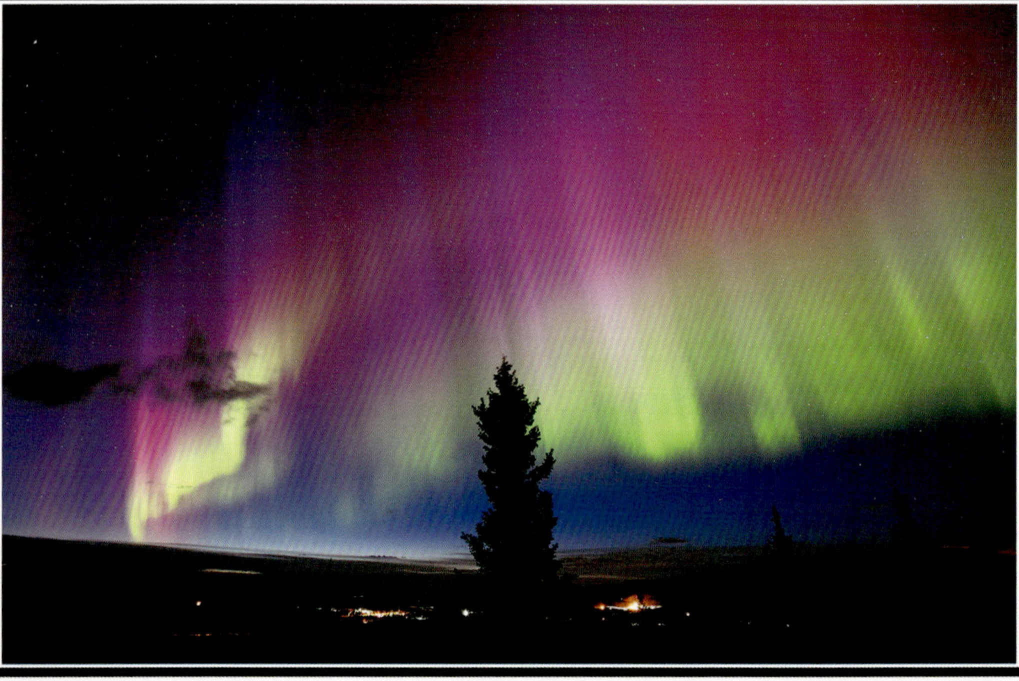

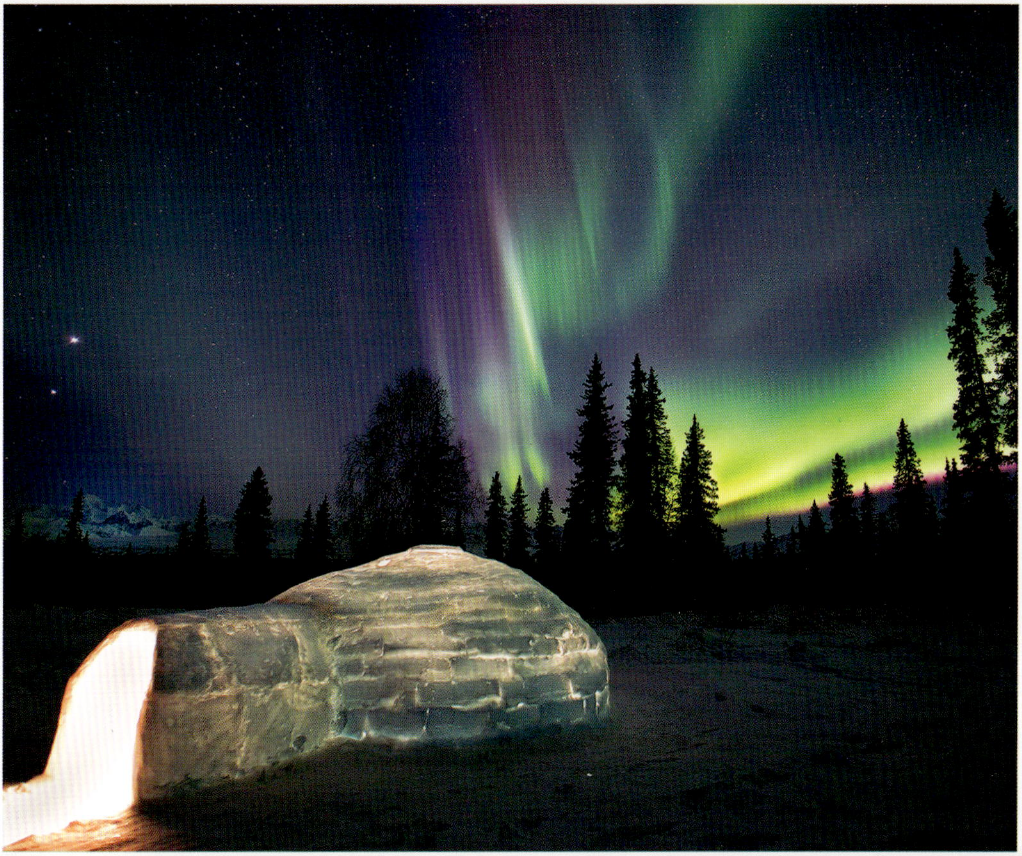

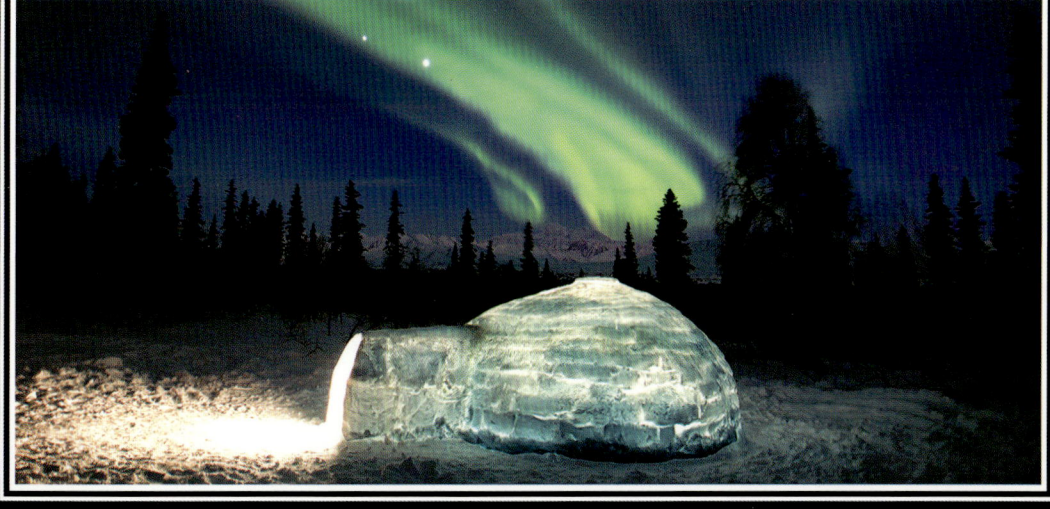

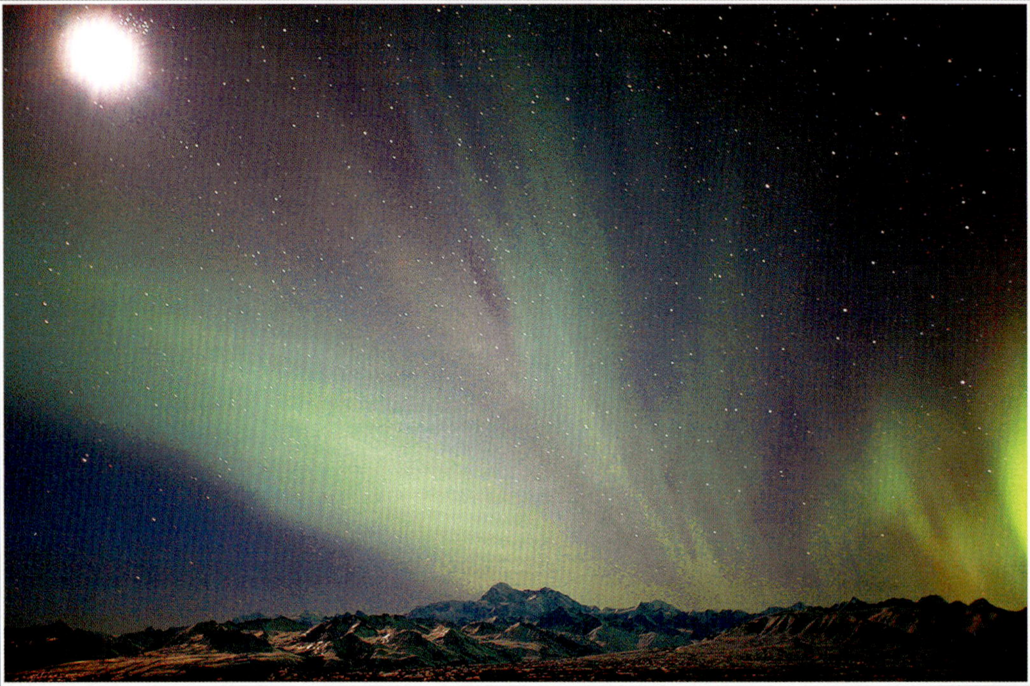

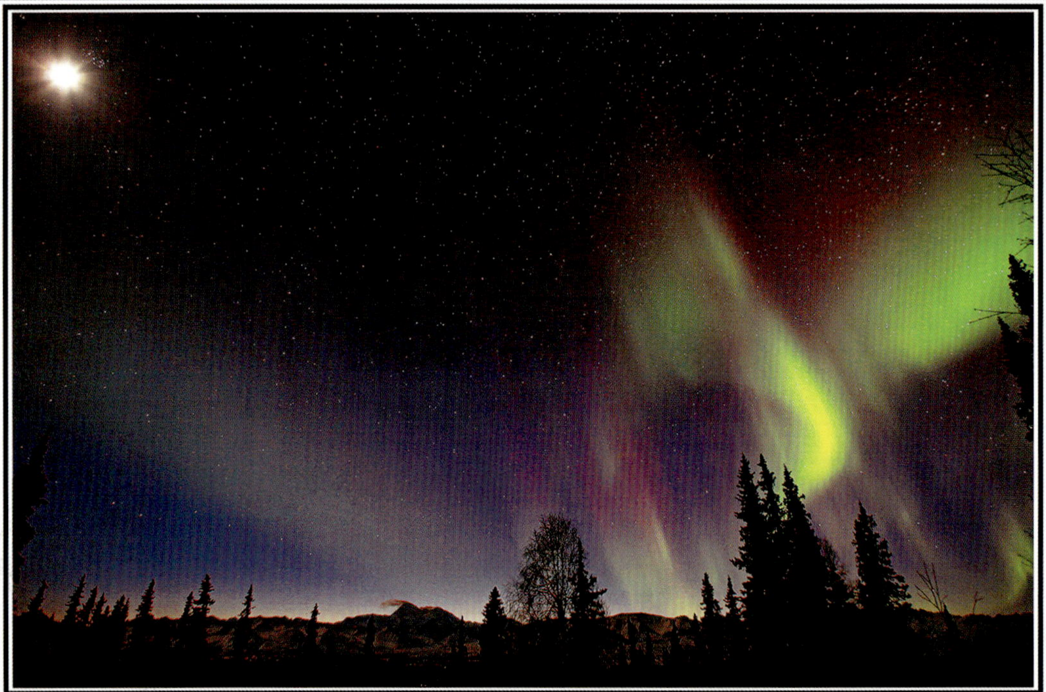

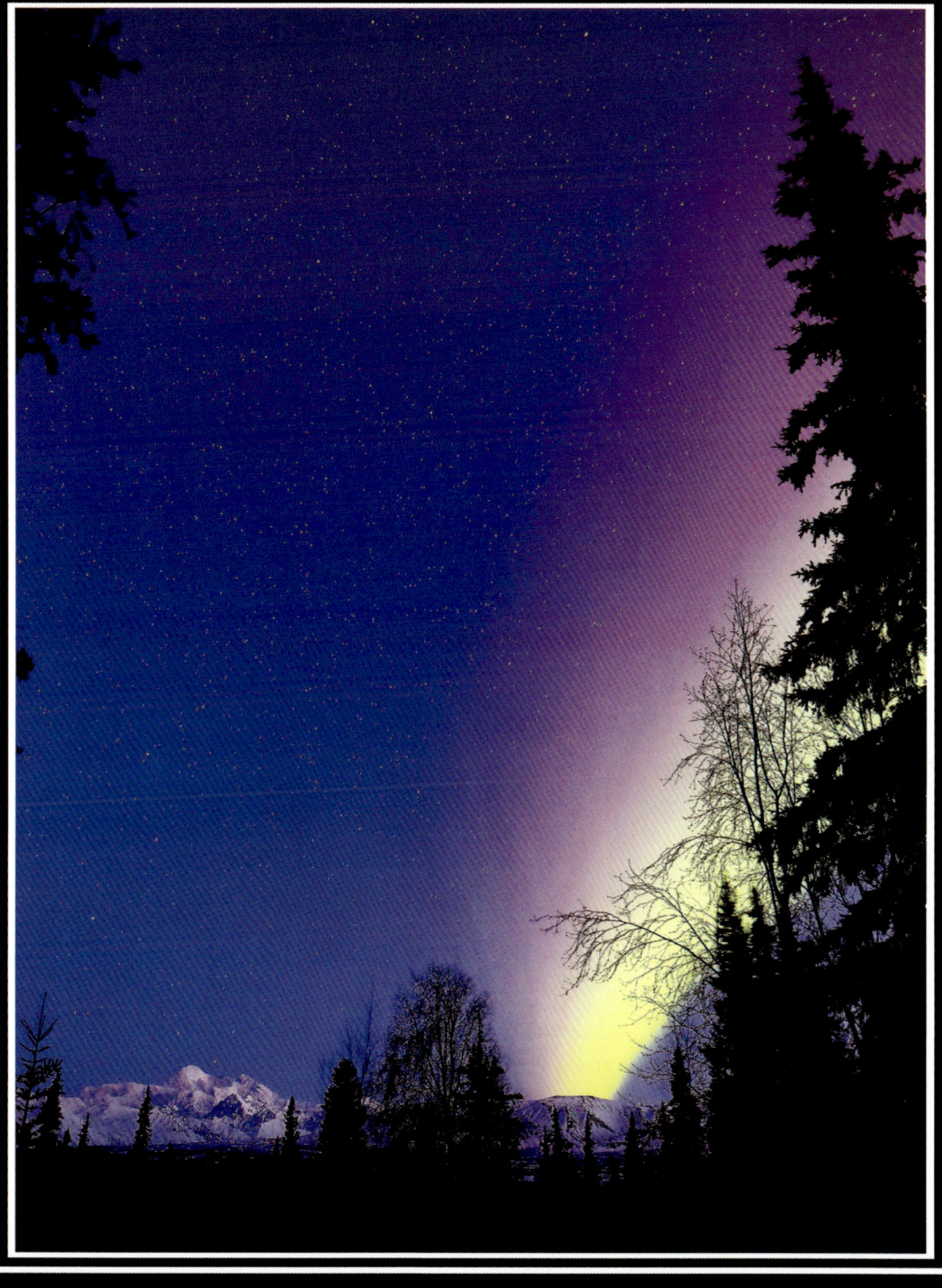

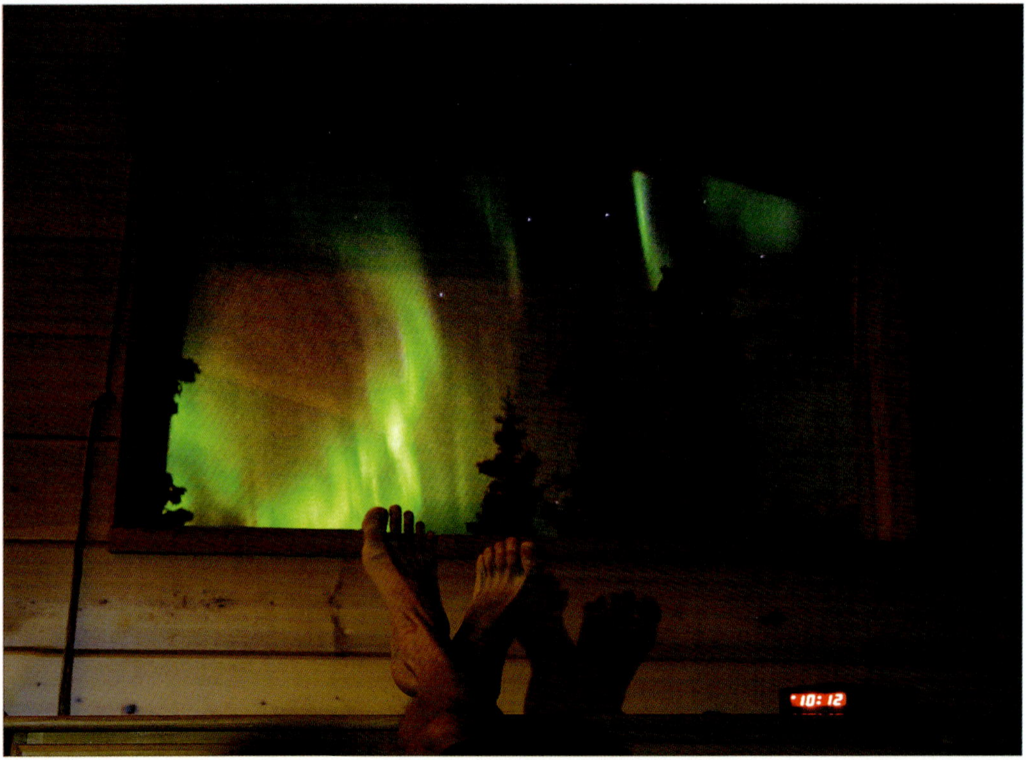

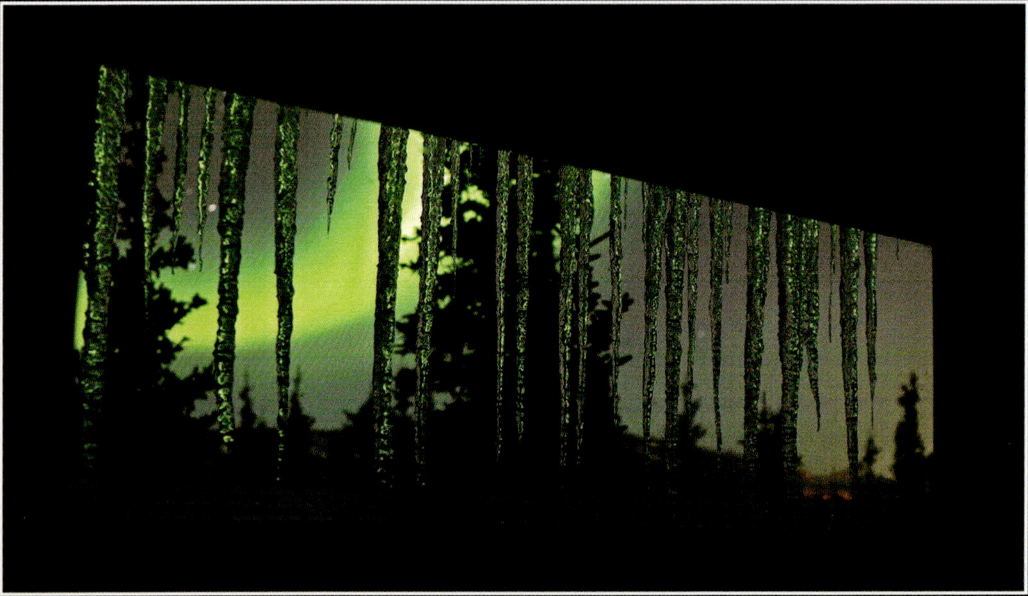

Dance of the Lights

I look out my northern window and see the aurora borealis start to dance.
I jump out of bed and put on my long johns, I throw on my extra warm pants.

I don my hat and neck gator and put on my moose mukluks too.
I slip on my down parka and mittens; I want to be warm while I take in the view.

I grab my cameras and tripods and head on out the front door
and look to the heavens above me to see what they have in store.

There's a shimmering band of deep purple and iridescent green;
the snow covered trees are all lit up by the full moon's bright glowing beam.

The shimmering band dances wildly across the awesome night sky.
The northern lights are intense tonight, the aurora is certainly not shy.

The lights start to pulsate rapidly straight over my laid back head
with green and purple and blue and several different shades of red.

As they pulsate they somewhat resemble a dove's open wings and its tail;
a shooting star streaks through the middle leaving a long and glistening trail.

My mustache is starting to freeze up because it is thirty two degrees below,
but I feel toasty warm and comfy under the aurora's sweet magical glow.

I dressed real warm and it pays off while standing out in the cold.
I can enjoy the aurora for hours as the light show continues to unfold.

The aurora borealis sizzles across the entire sky filled with stars.
The colorful curtains of light dance in front of Jupiter, Venus and Mars.

Each moment is so very different, eye opening and unique as can be.
When the aurora is active like this, it's overwhelming, there's so much to see.

Streaks and curtains and ovals of brilliant colors of light,
enchanting angelic auroral wings that enliven and light up the night.

Dance of the Lights

Getting a good photo is secondary to experiencing this mystical feat,
but to share amazing images of this, to many, is a breathtaking treat.

As a splendid service to others, I aim, I focus and shoot.
As I wait for the long exposure, I gaze up at the sky and hoot.

I hoot at the moon and the stars and the dazzling northern lights.
There is nothing quite like Alaska's cold and quiet, long winter nights.

It sounds pretty scary to many but it has a specially rewarding allure;
watching the dance of the lights in the winter is simply spectacular, that's for sure!

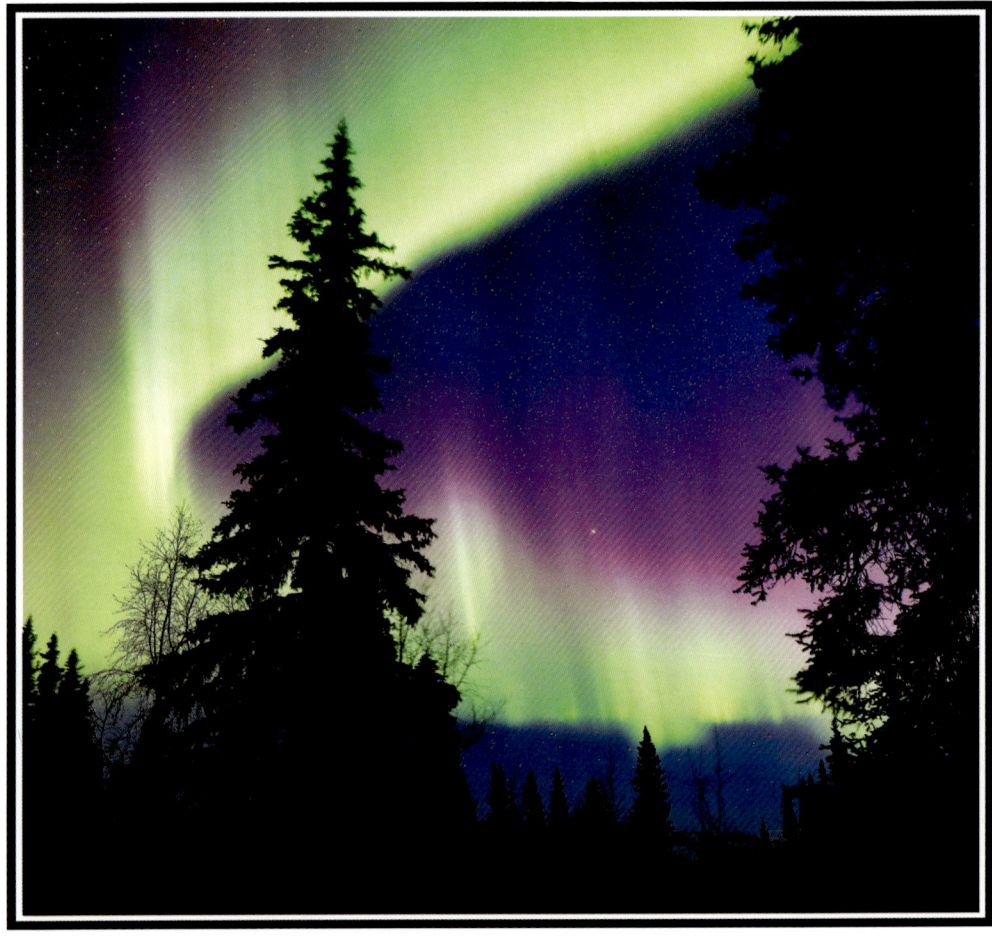

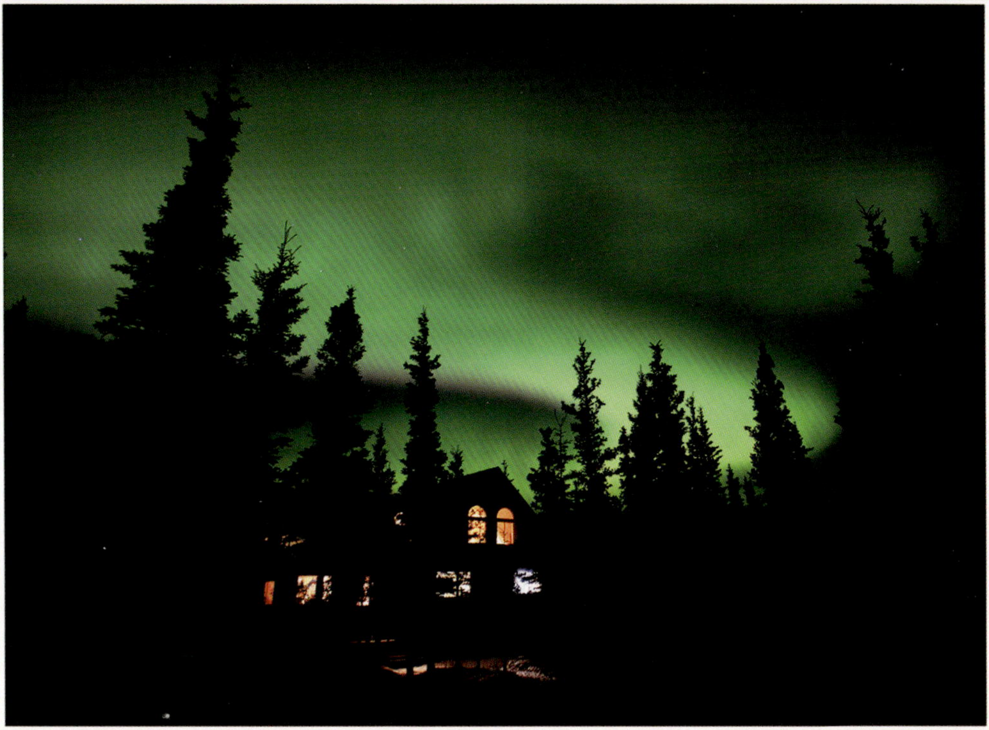

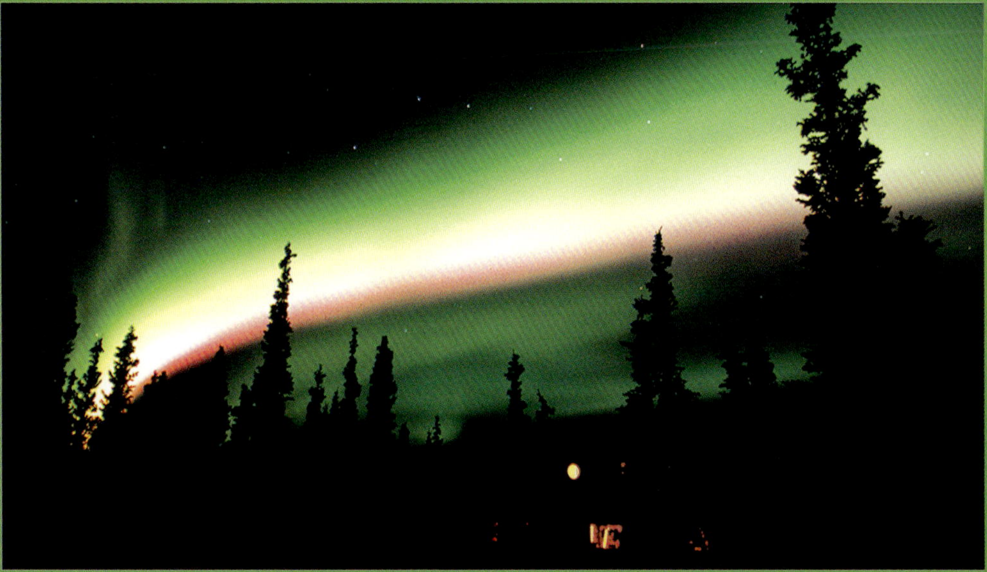

23

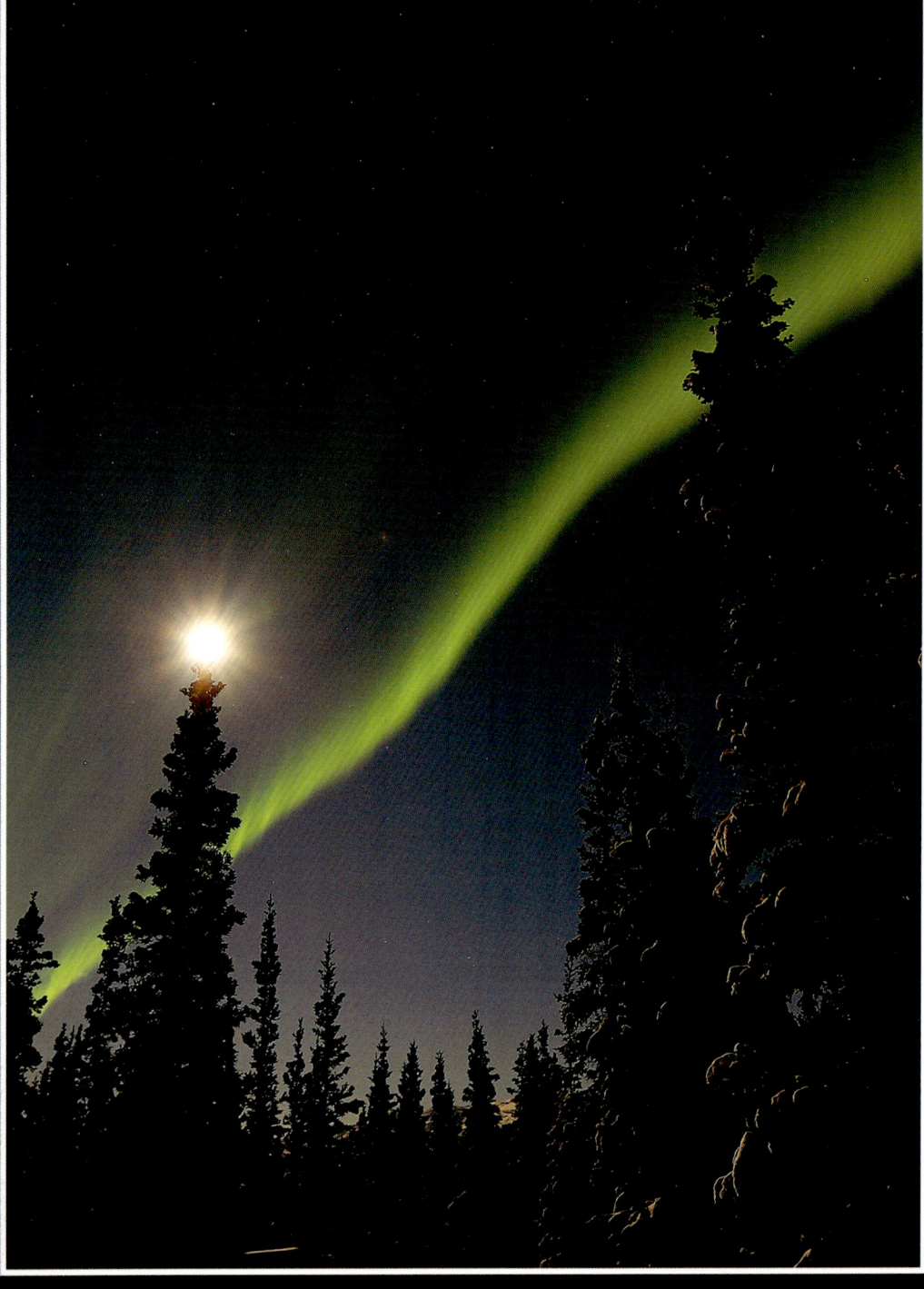

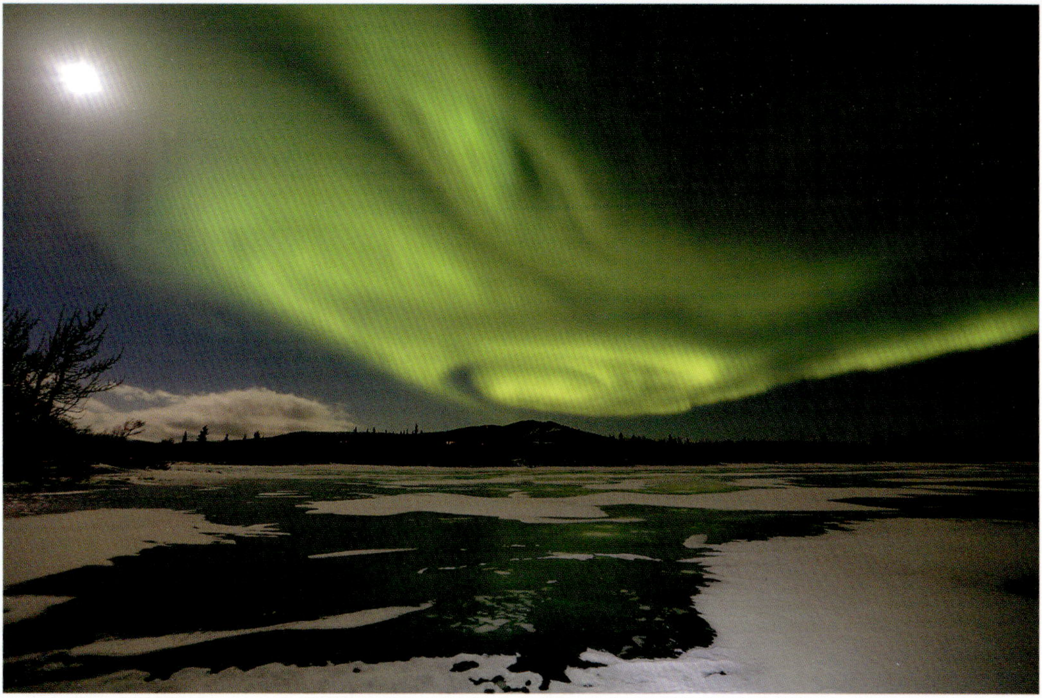

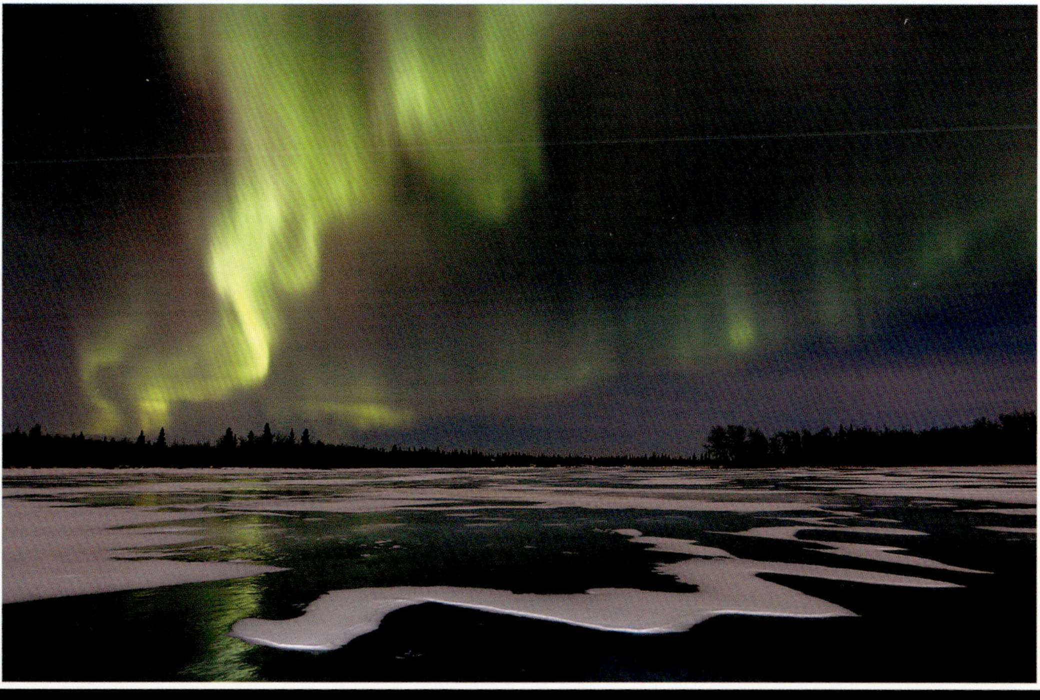

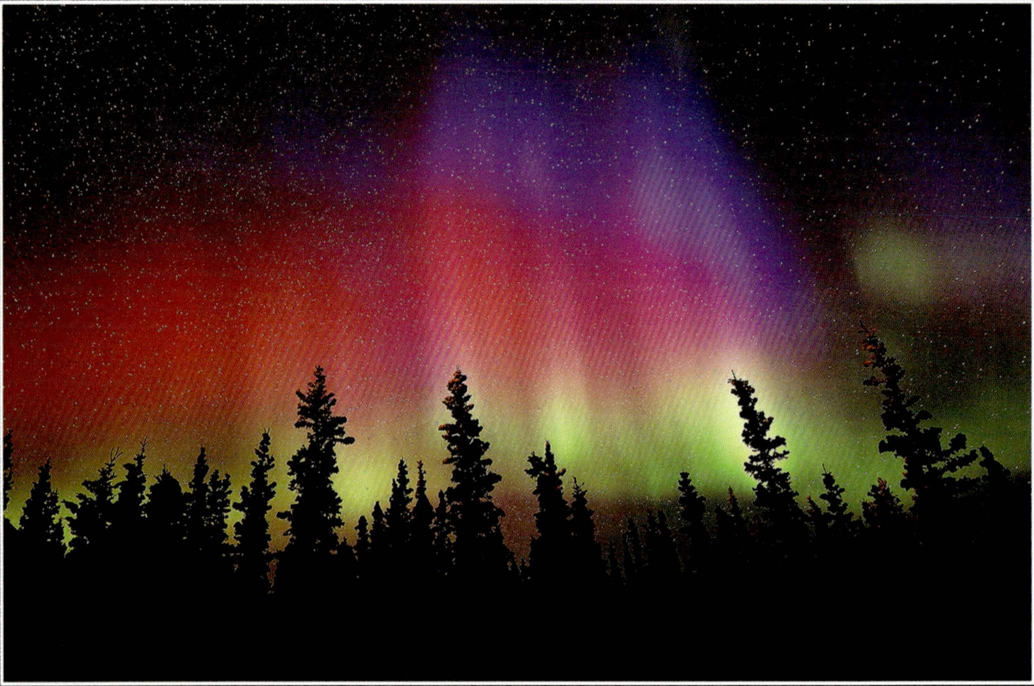

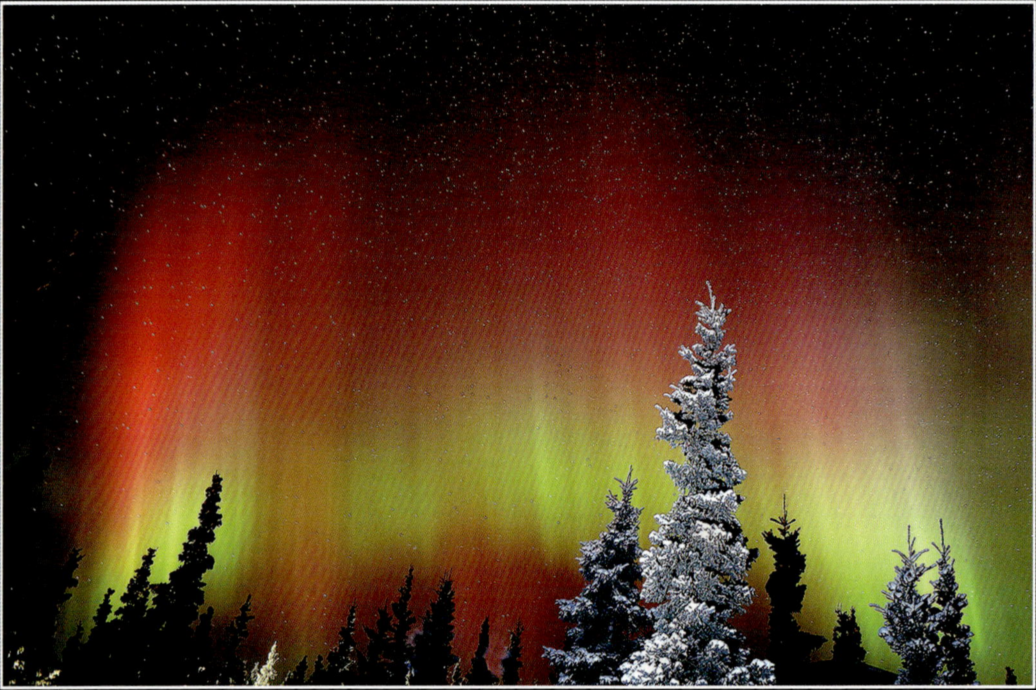

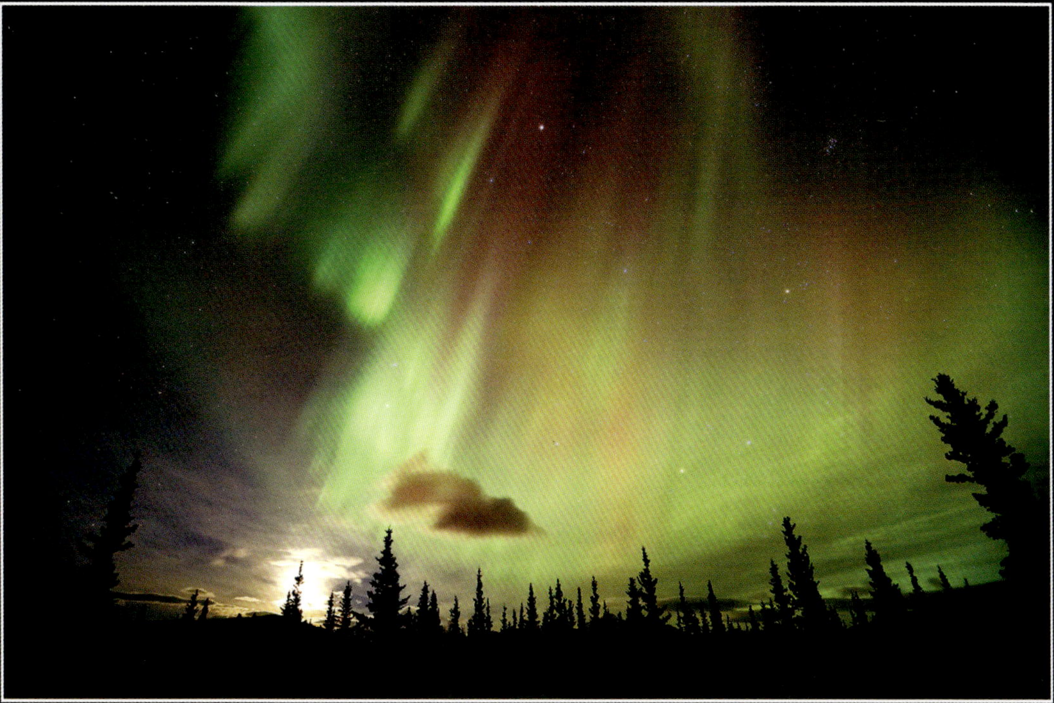

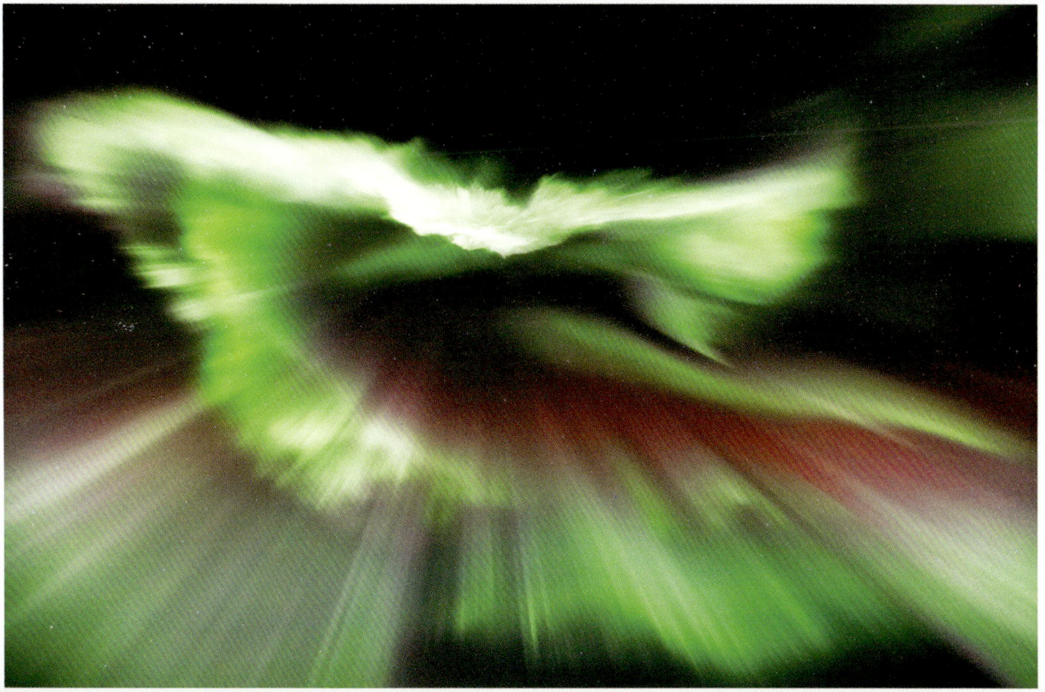

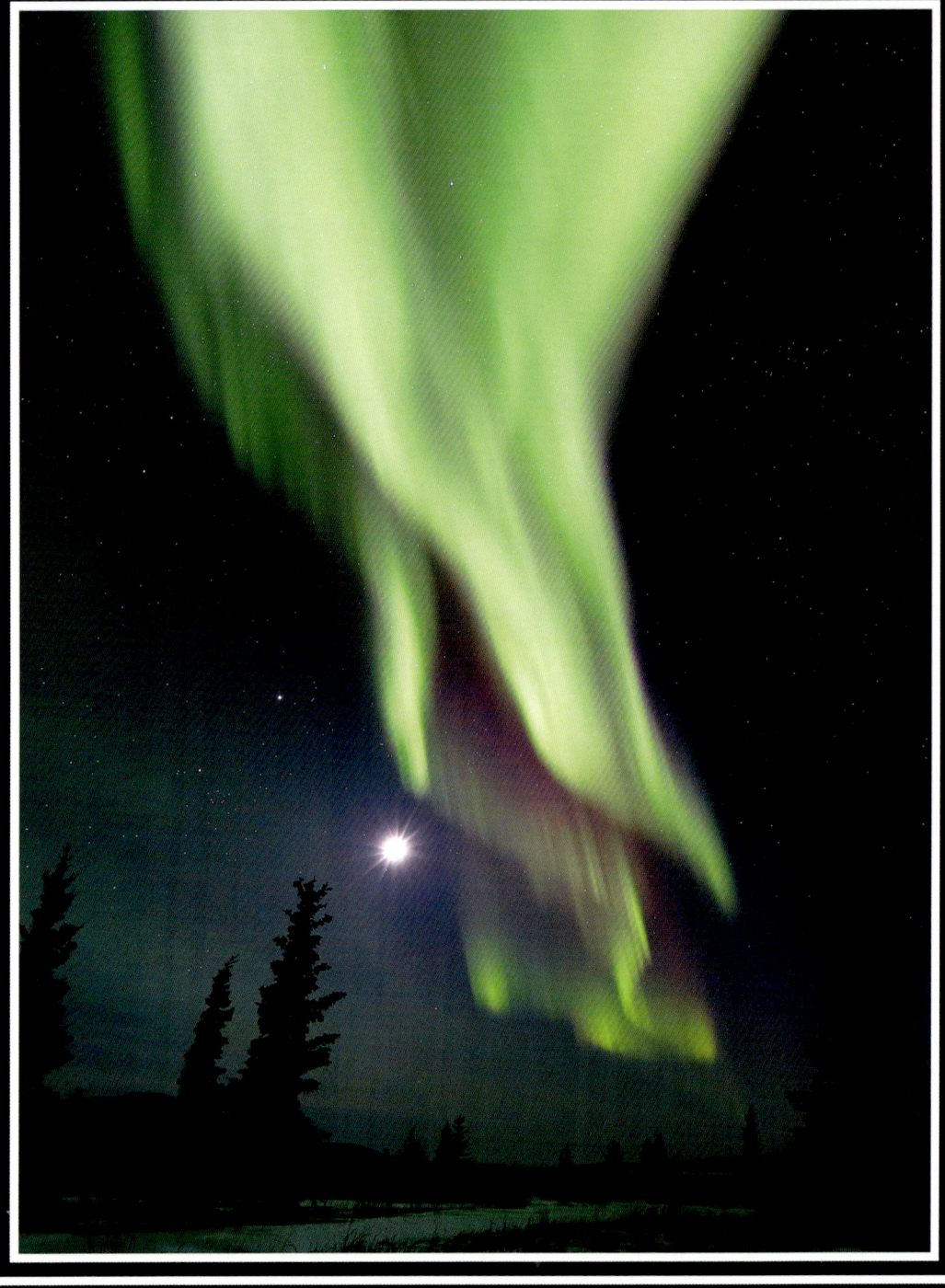

Cold and Dark

The snow is piling up and the food is getting thin;
soon all of the bears will be holed up in their den.
The temperature is dropping and the animals all know
that this is the season that is dominated by snow.
Most birds fly south and most people as well;
for many, an Alaskan winter is a living hell.
There are some animals and people that thrive as they should
when the land turns to white and the living is good.
The lynx, the wolf, the snowshoe hare,
the fox, the moose, the caribou all share
the beauty you find in the short winter days;
it's harsh but it's sweet in so many ways.
The hustle of summer is gone with the winds.
Now people have time to share with their friends.
The light might not be long but the quality is there,
the beautiful soft hues you just can't compare.
The solitude, the pureness, the essence of being,
stick around in the winter and that's what you'll be seeing.
Along with the dance of the northern lights show
you'll experience some things that will sure make you grow.
At forty below you learn to be ready;
it makes you tough, humble and steady.
Just watch the Dall sheep up in the high places;
they're the toughest animals with the most peaceful faces.
The raven, the magpie and the gray jay
are three hearty birds that manage to stay.
There's not much food but the competition is thin,
and that alone is a big reason to grin.
People will often ask "isn't it just cold and dark?"
Look into an Alaskan's eyes and you will see the spark.
The highways are empty but our hearts are full,
the winter in Alaska has a mystical pull.
It's a pull that many will never quite see;
it's cold, it's dark but it's ever so free.
Cars don't want to start so you have to plug in.
With the clothes you must wear no one looks thin.

Cold and Dark

When it gets colder than thirty below,
cover up good, don't let your skin show;
because frostbite will get you if you're not prepared.
It's only the foolish that tend to get scared.
If you learn to be wise and know all the tricks
it's quite enjoyable cruisin' around in the sticks.
There's snow to play in and ice all around.
It's amazing the distance of the travel of sound.
Propane stays liquid at about fifty below,
you must heat your tank if you want it to flow.
At these temps you can throw hot water that's wet
and ice fog and snow is all that you'll get.
The cold, it does some very interesting things
as the aurora dances overhead with it's angelic wings.
There is a beauty in the harshness I will have to say,
it's cold and dark and I like it that way.

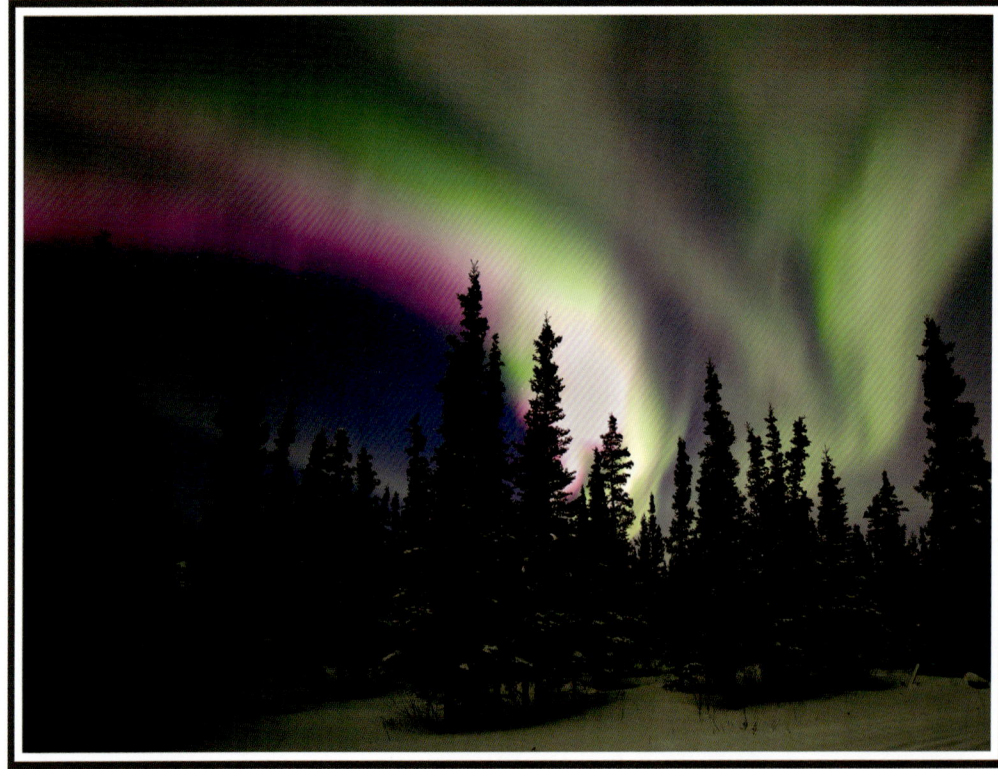

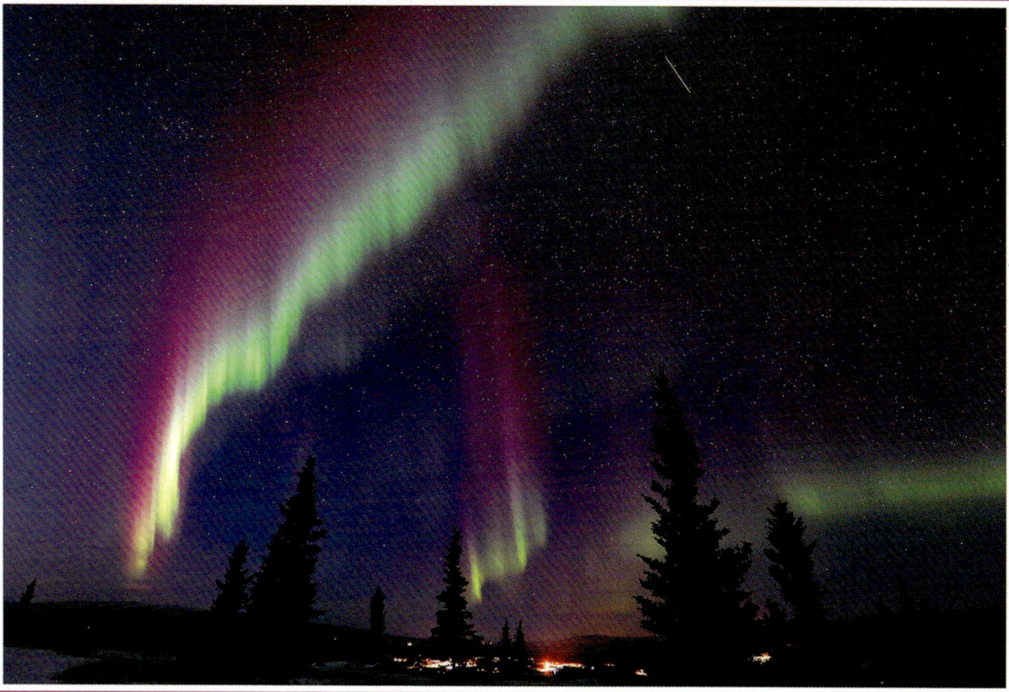

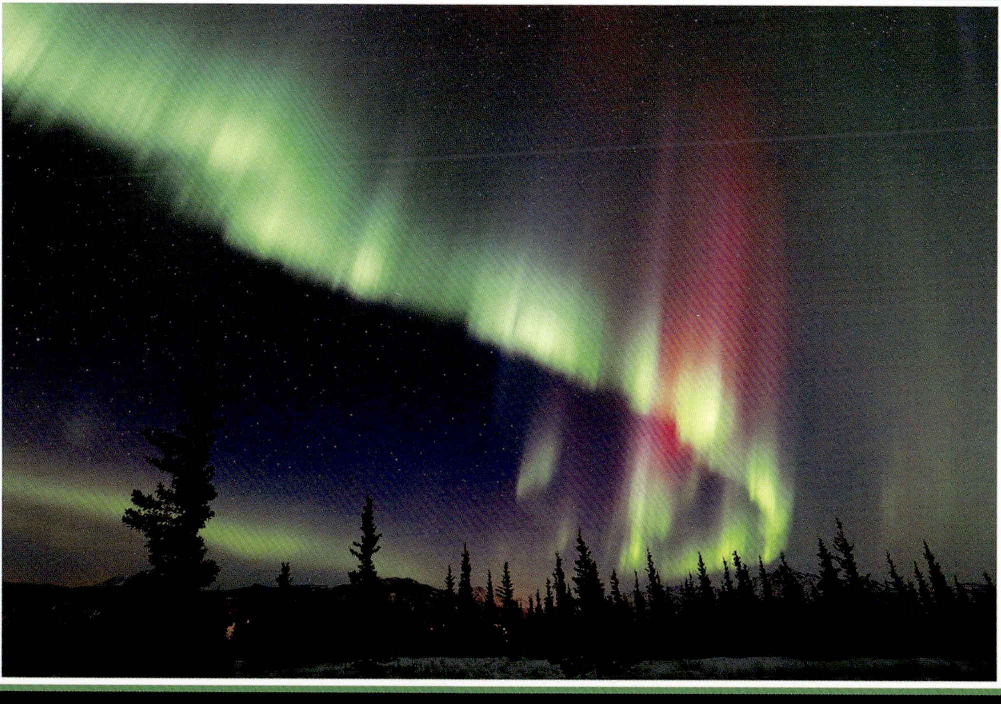

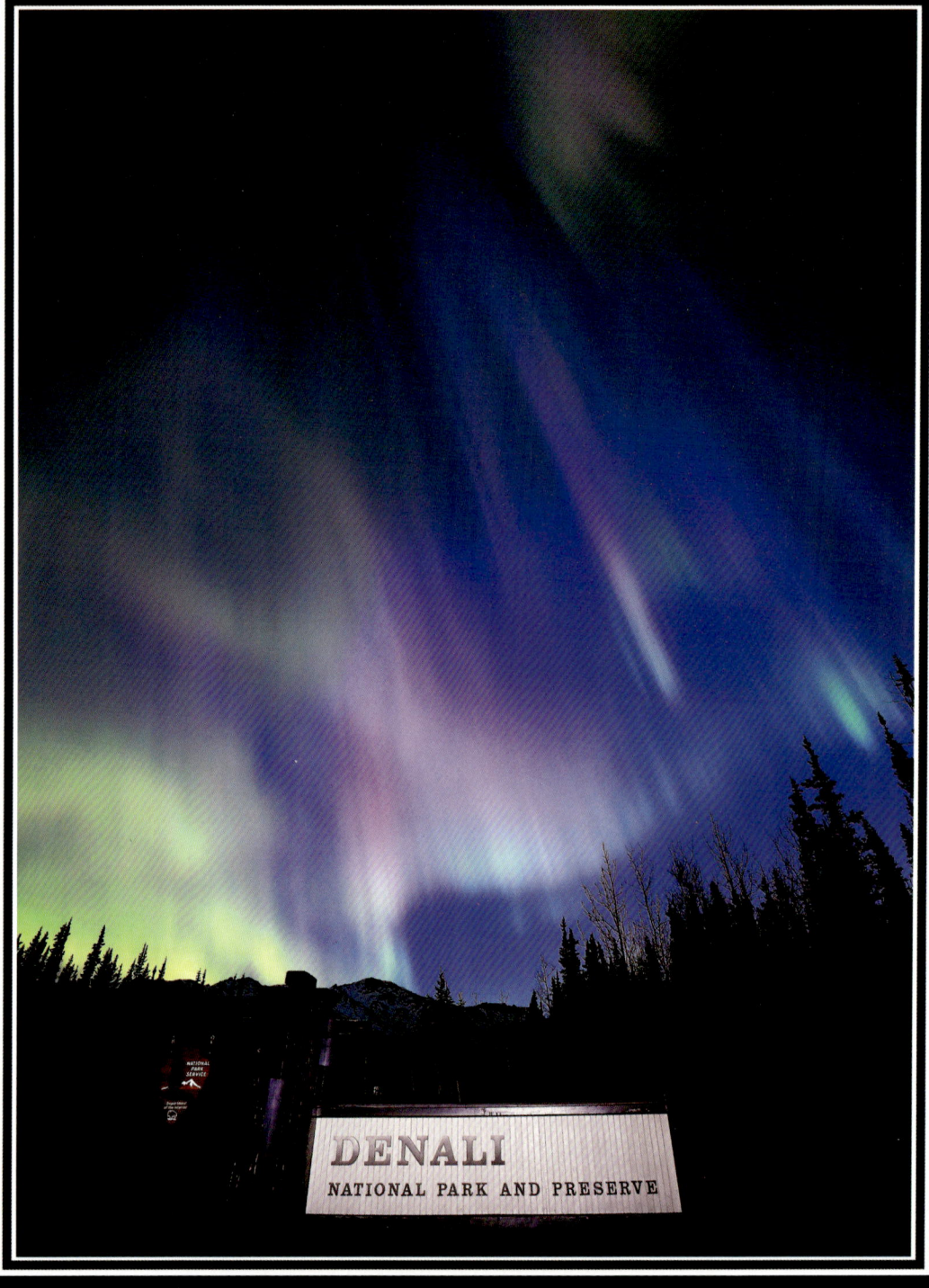

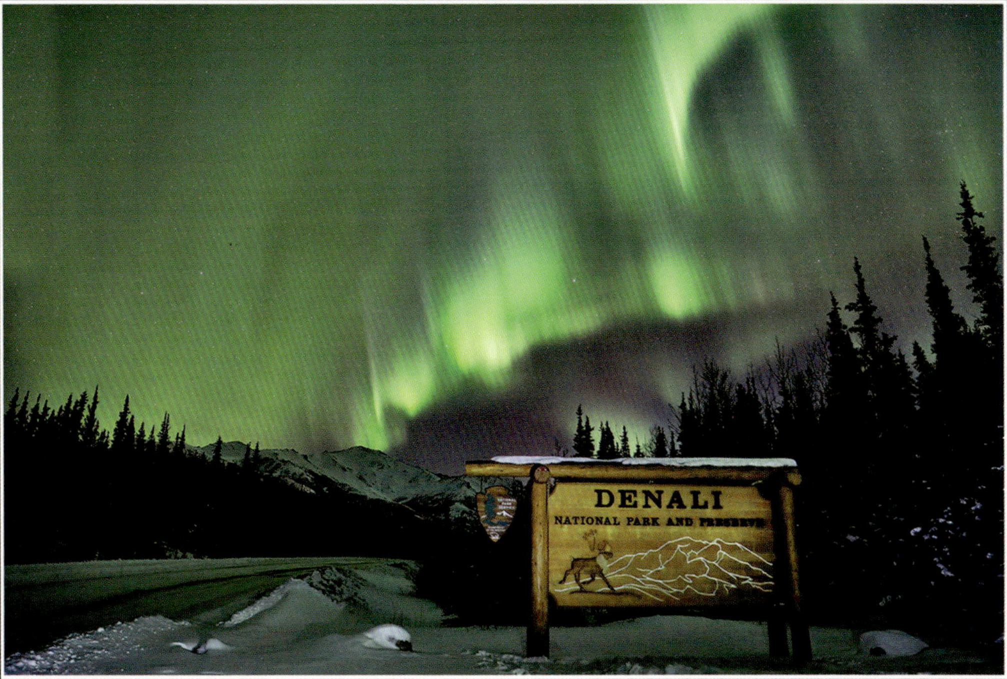

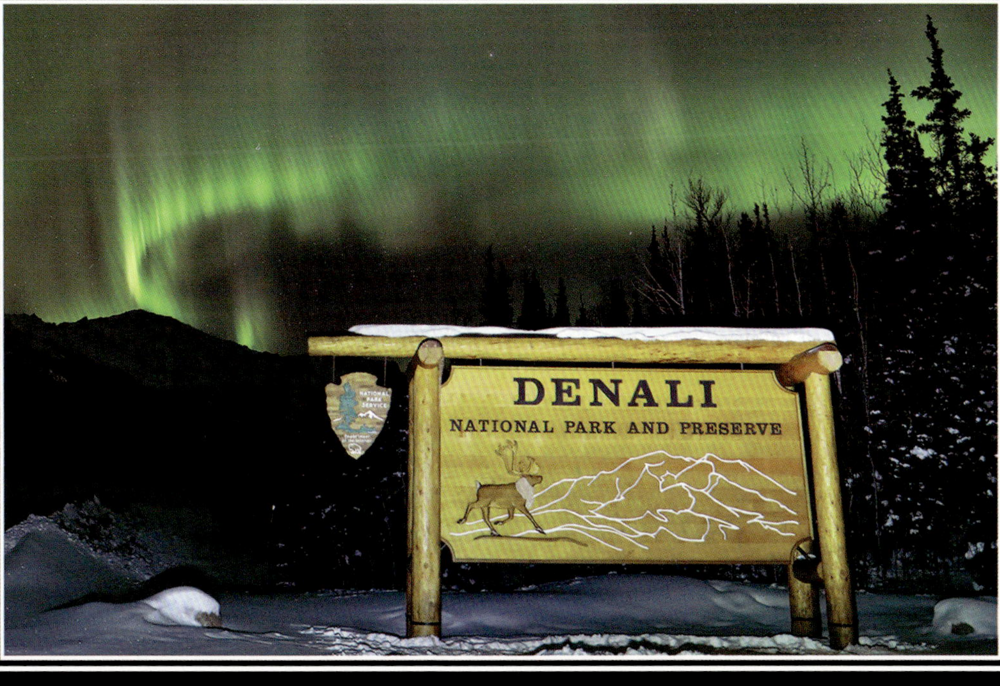

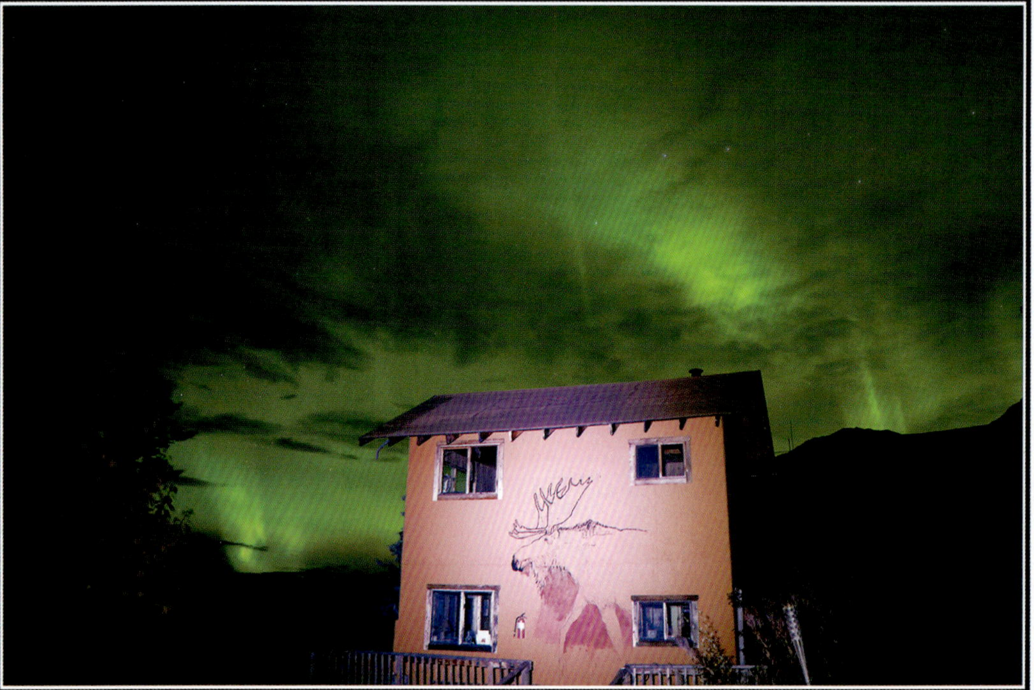

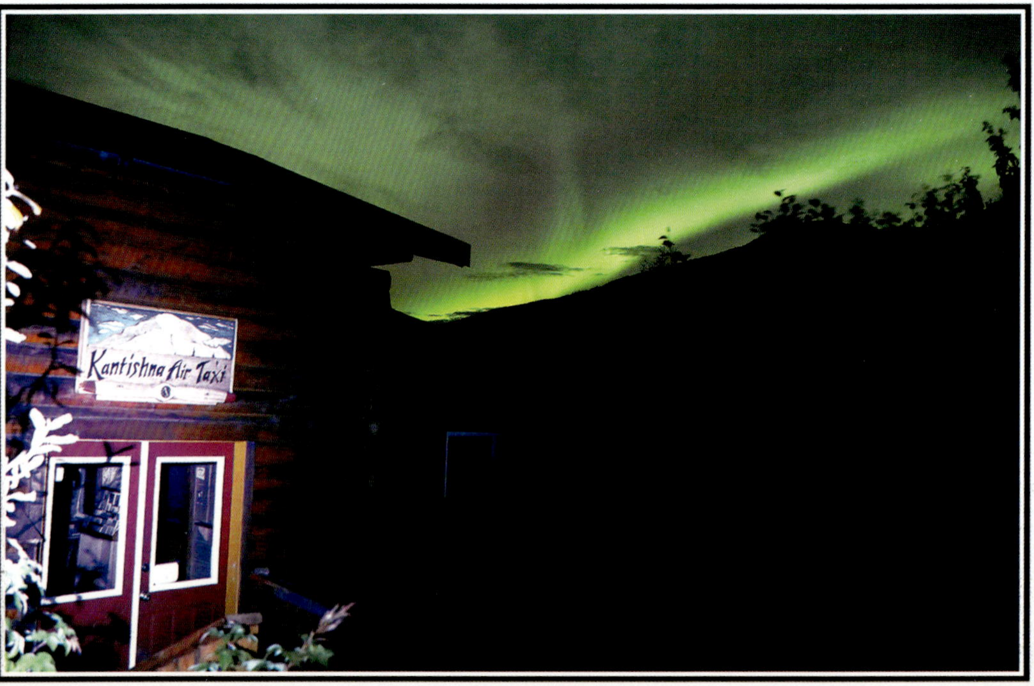

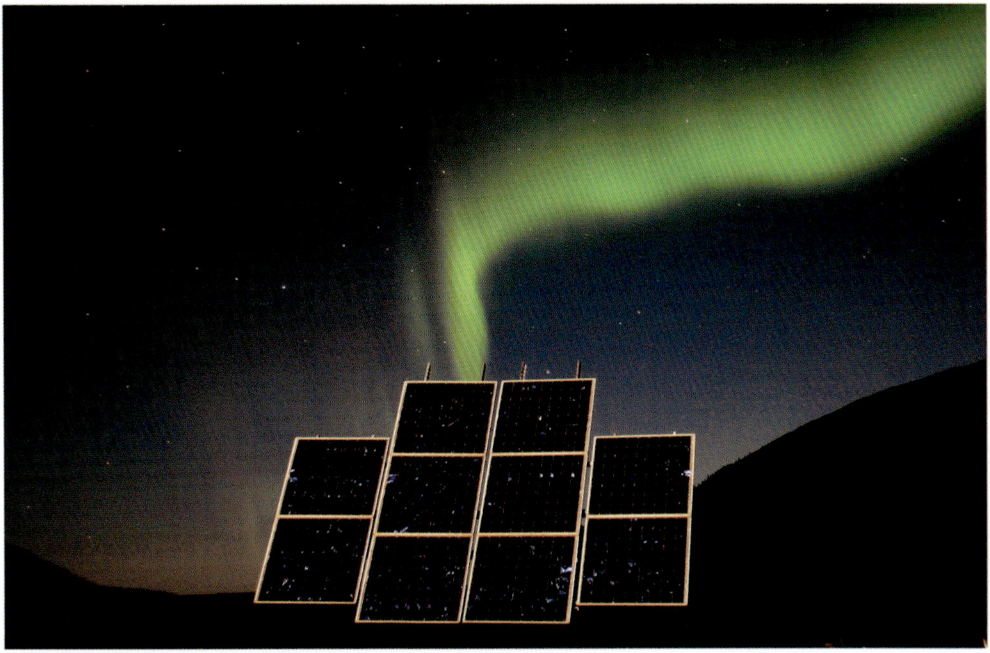

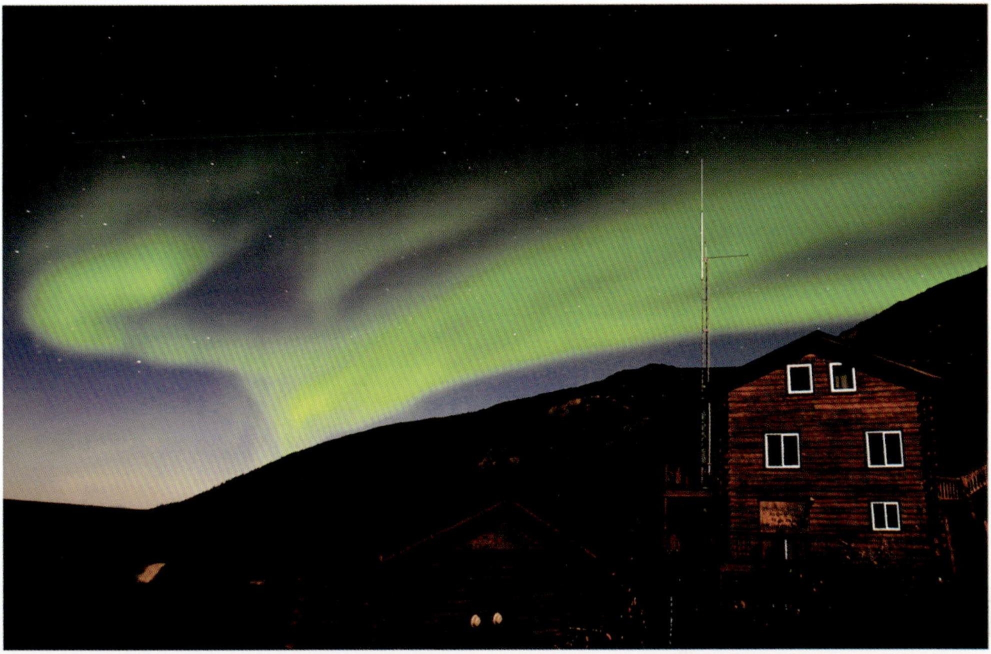

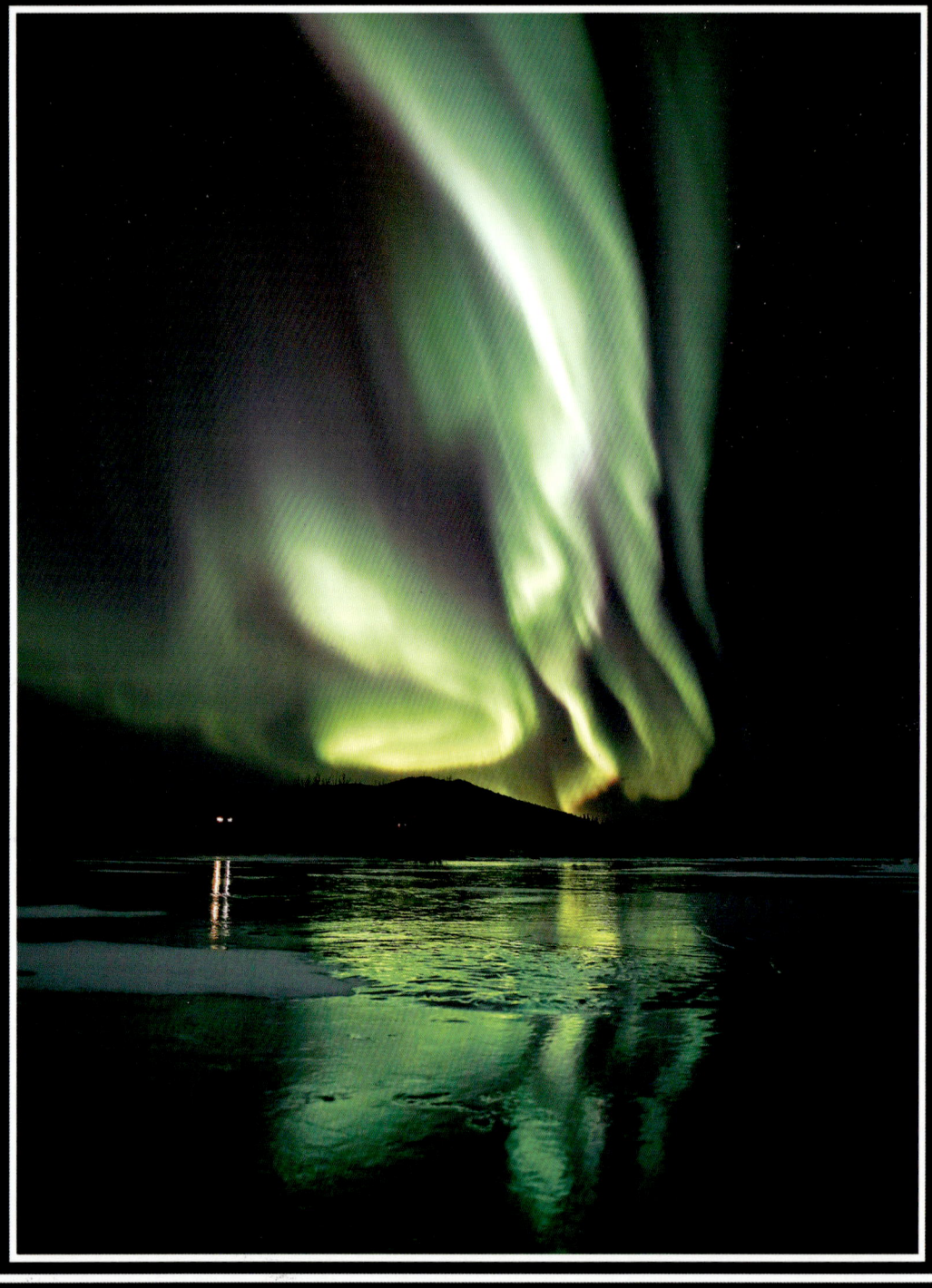

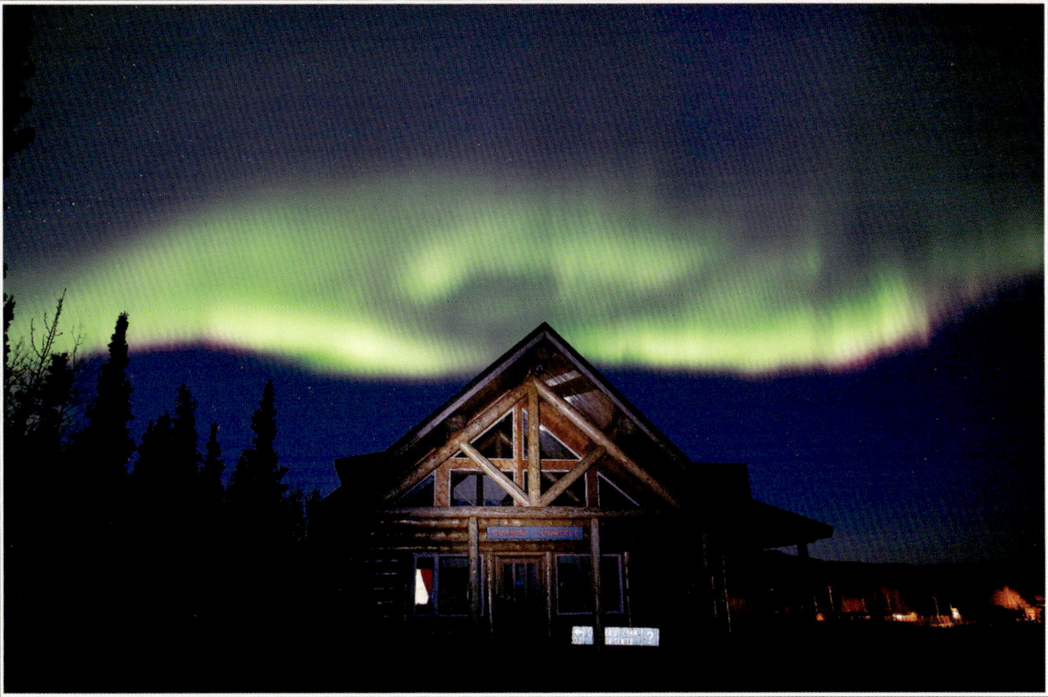

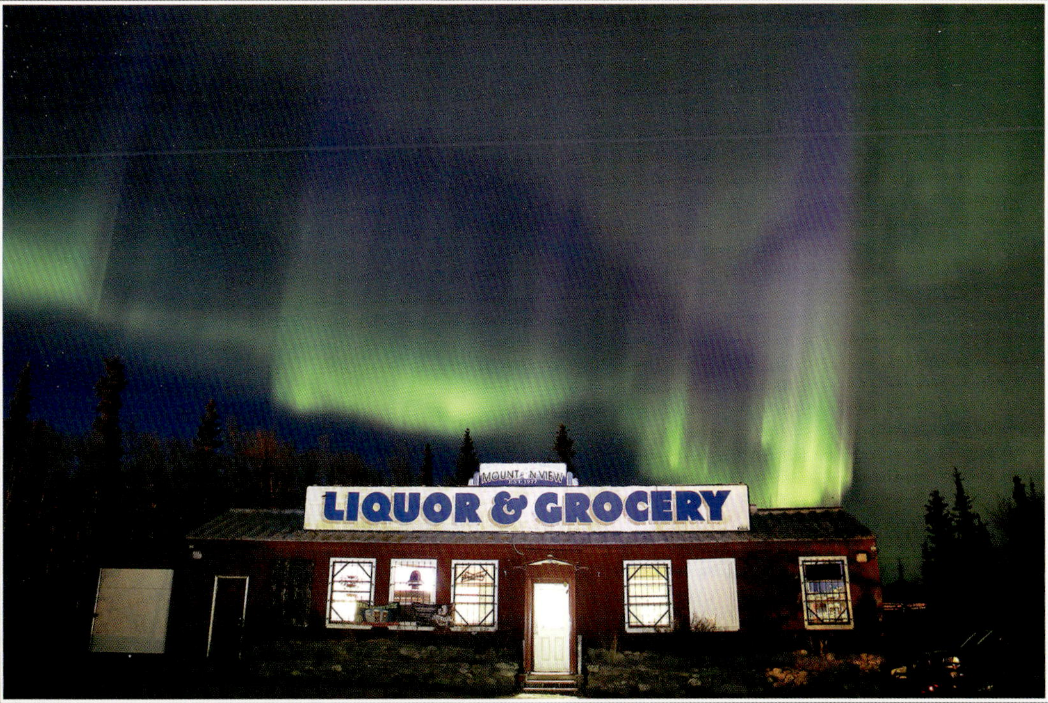

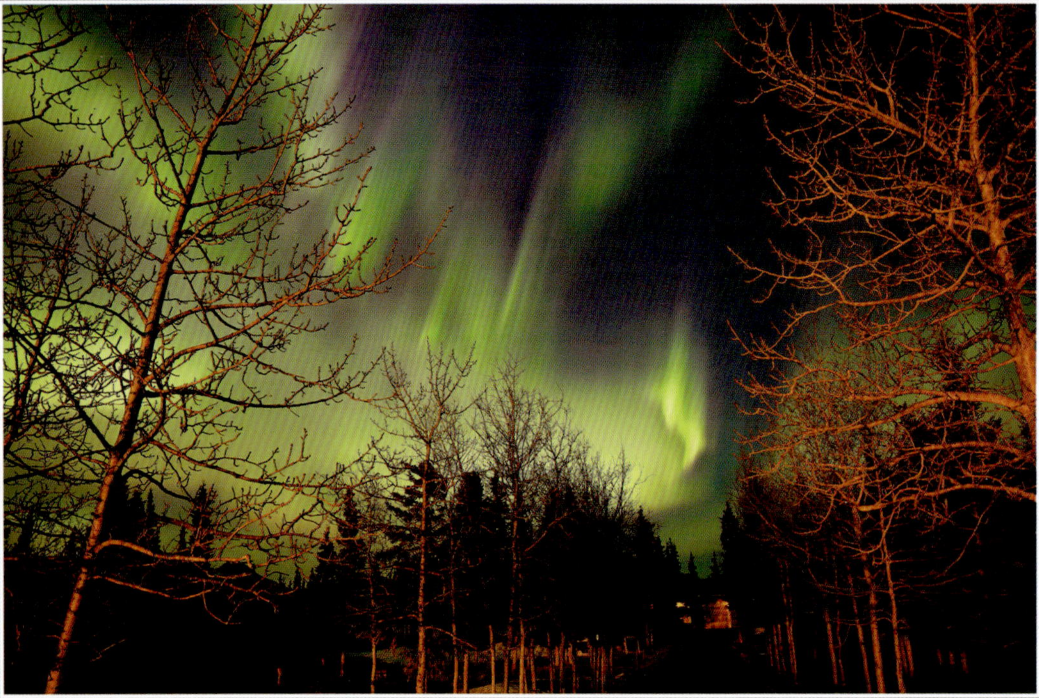

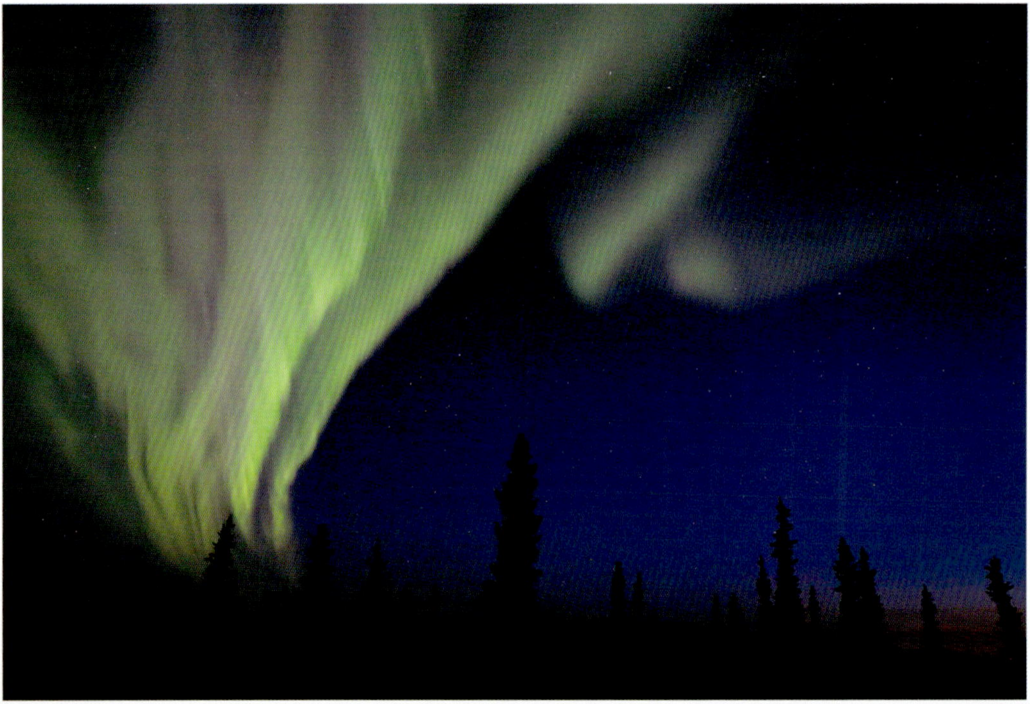

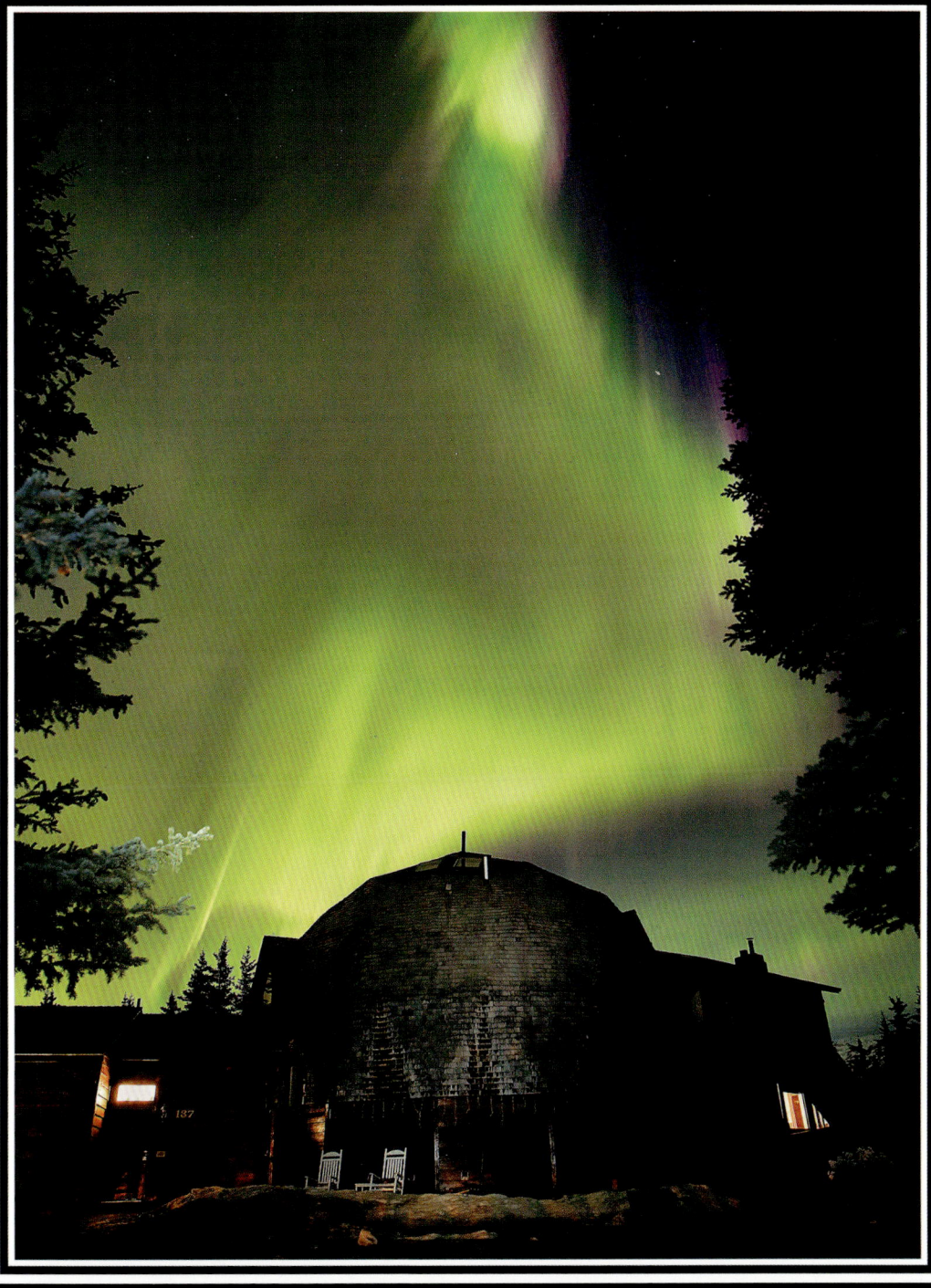

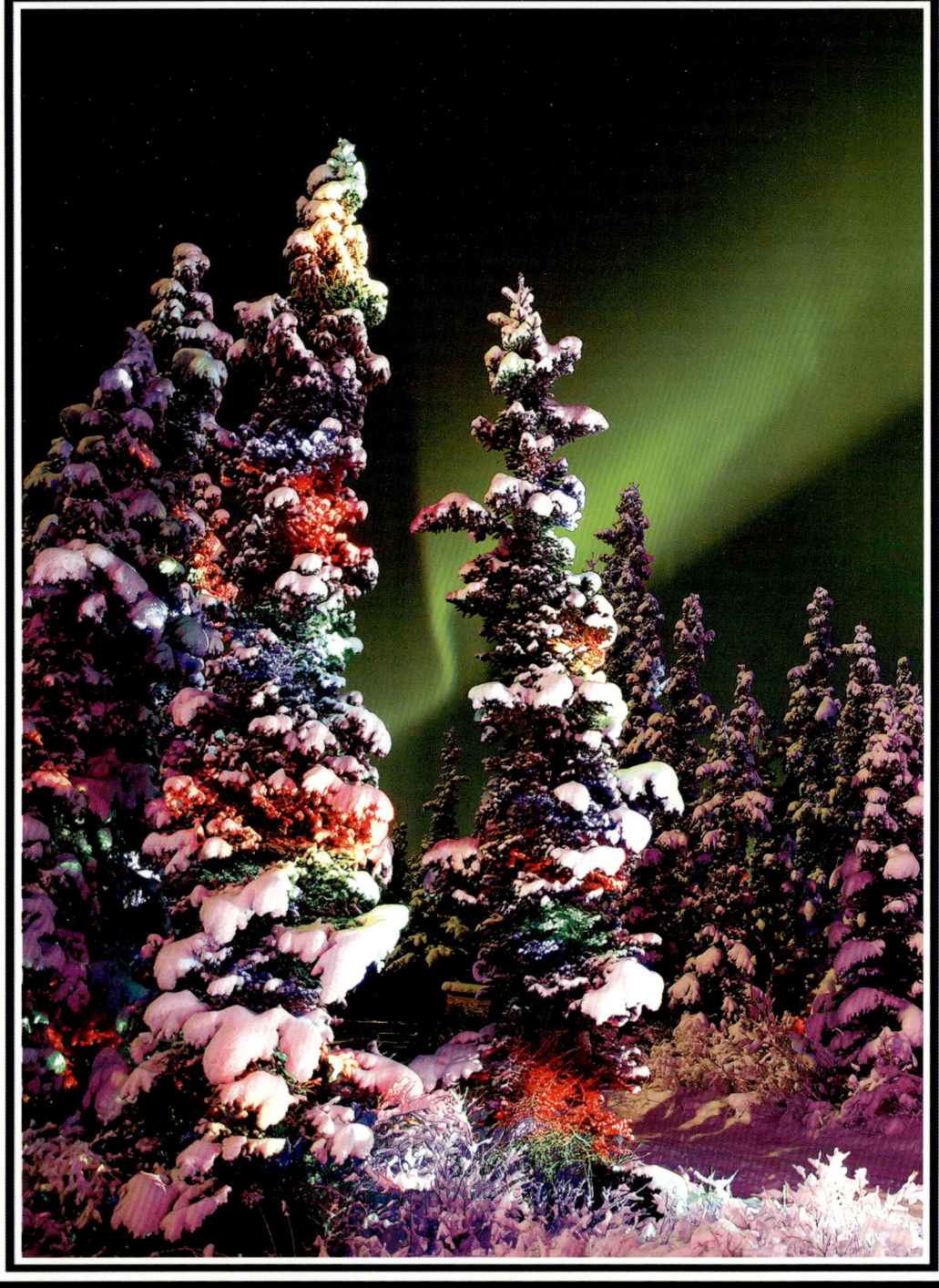

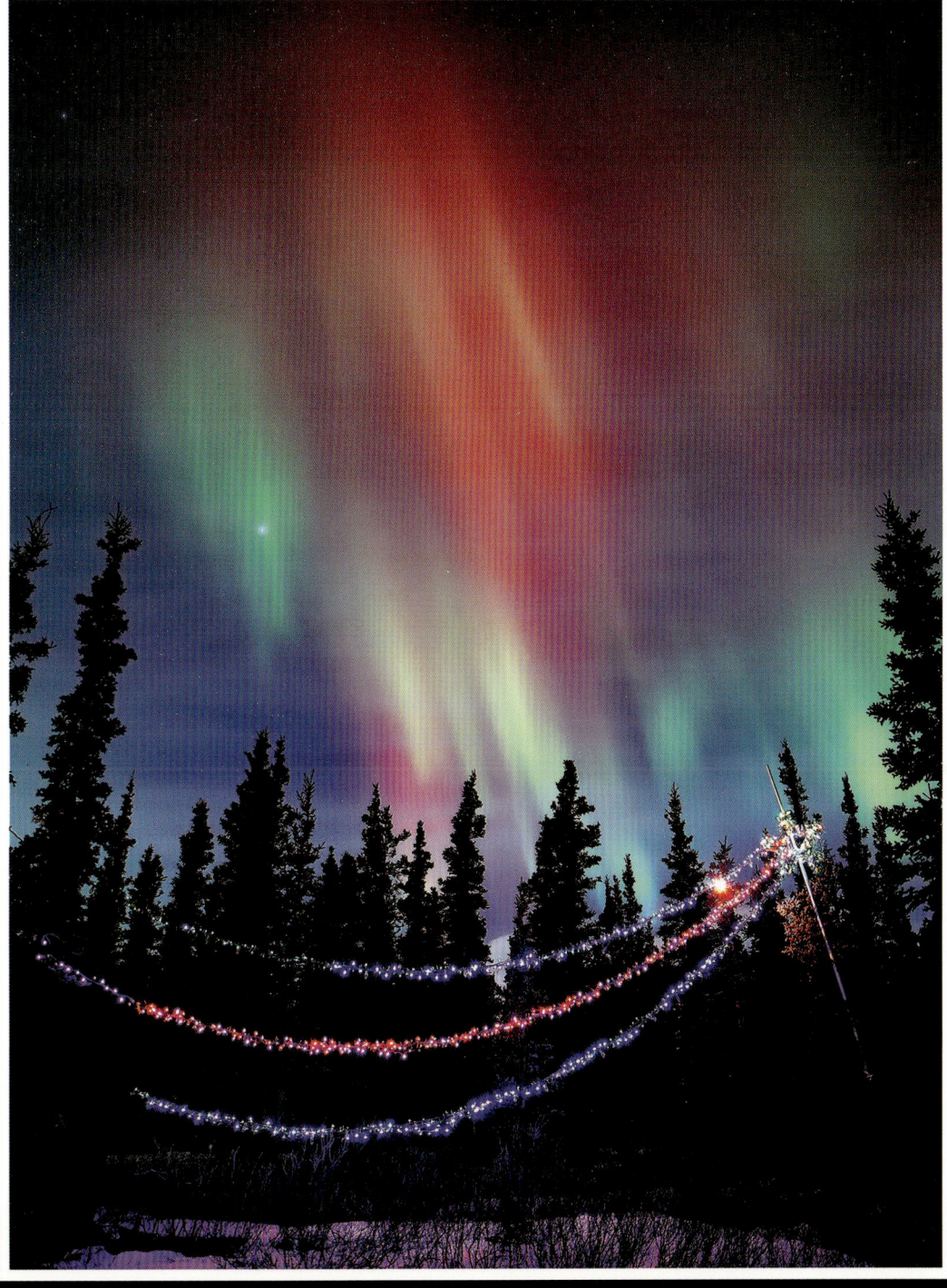

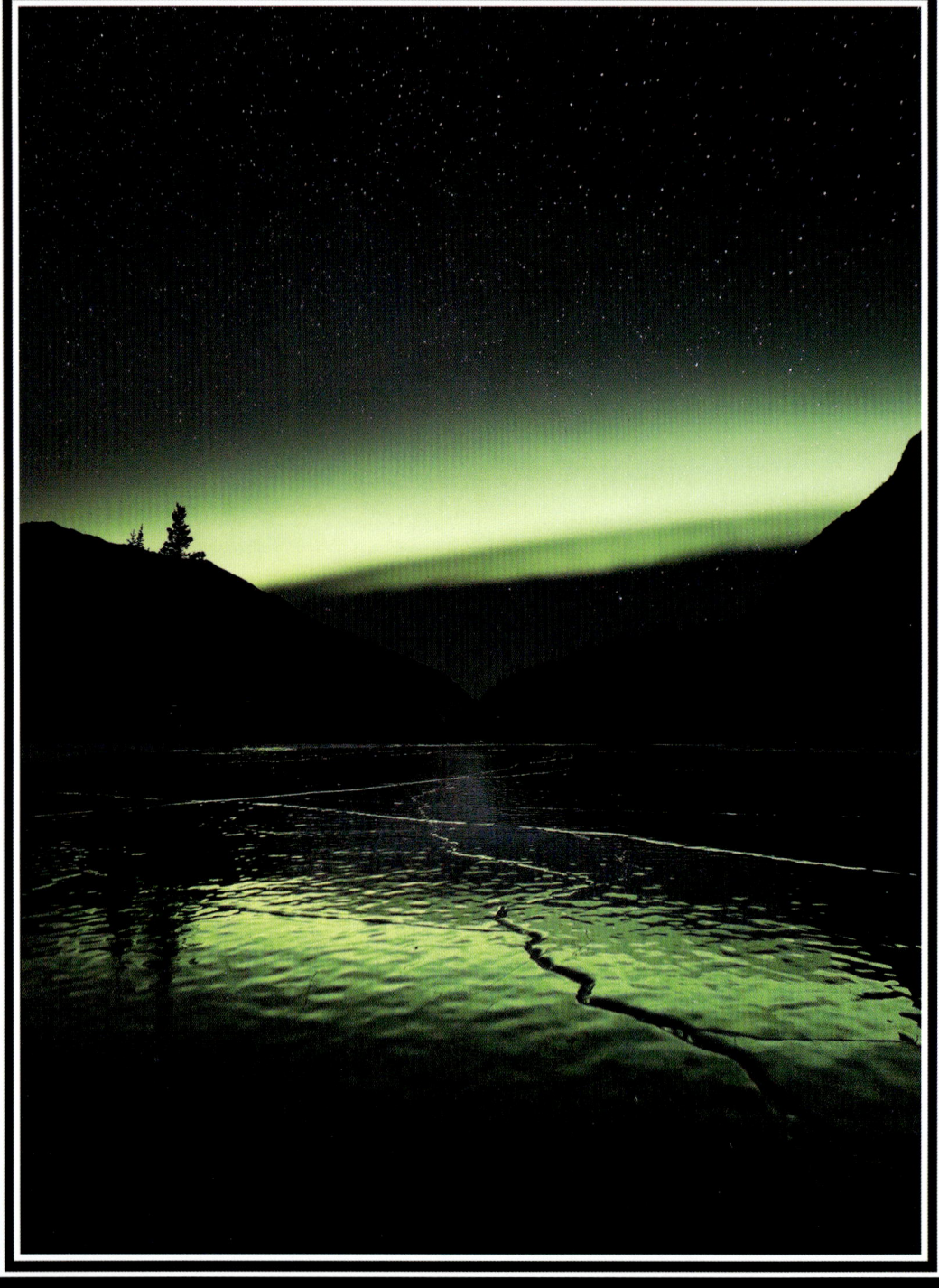

An Awakening of Light

I was laying on my back on the glare ice of a cold, hard frozen, clear lake
listening to the hoots of a great gray owl as the aurora began to awake.

There was a band of green light glowing and getting brighter and brighter quite fast.
It turned into curtains of brilliant light dancing across the night sky so vast.

There were pinks and purples and yellows, several different shades of red.
It made me feel like dancing along, so I got up off of my cold icy bed.

The light show was filling the sky to the north, the south, the east and the west.
I started shooting photos in all directions; I was astonished and certainly impressed.

On occasion the aurora was so bright that it seemed like the middle of the day.
There were swirling curtains and ovals of colors; there was no wind but it blew me away.

I was out on the ice for six hours and the intensity would come and would go.
With flares of light pulsating off and on, it was definitely a dazzling light show.

The streaks of light were reflected off of the smooth ice that was under my feet.
With a flash of my headlamp I captured images of the cracks in the ice that were neat.

I was amazed at the photos I was getting of the ice cracks, the reflections and the lights.
Standing in the middle of a frozen lake in silence, this was one of the most memorable
of all of my nights.

Experiencing the northern lights streaming through the sky like this and seeing them
brightly aflame
awakened a special place so deep in my soul and I will never be quite the same.

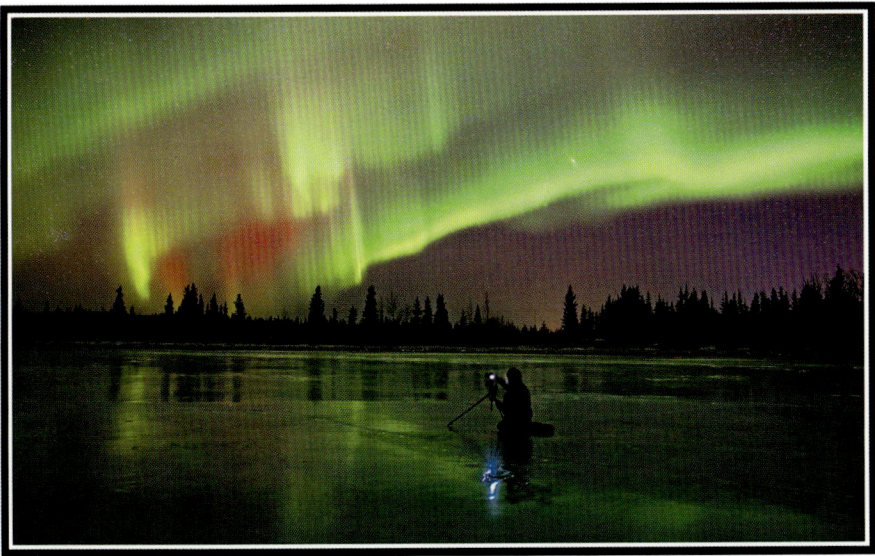

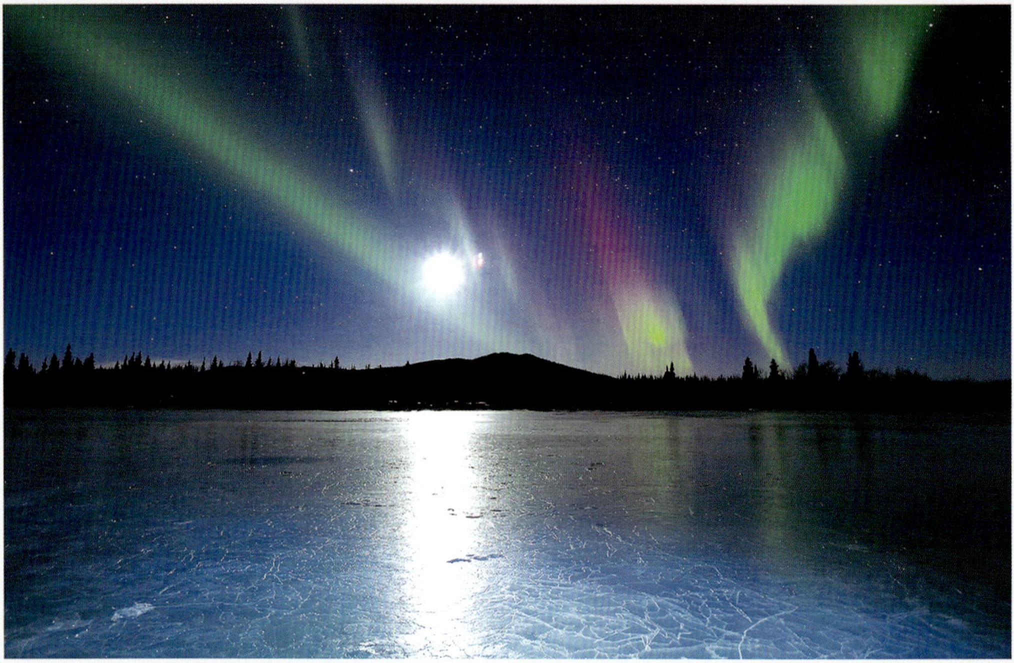

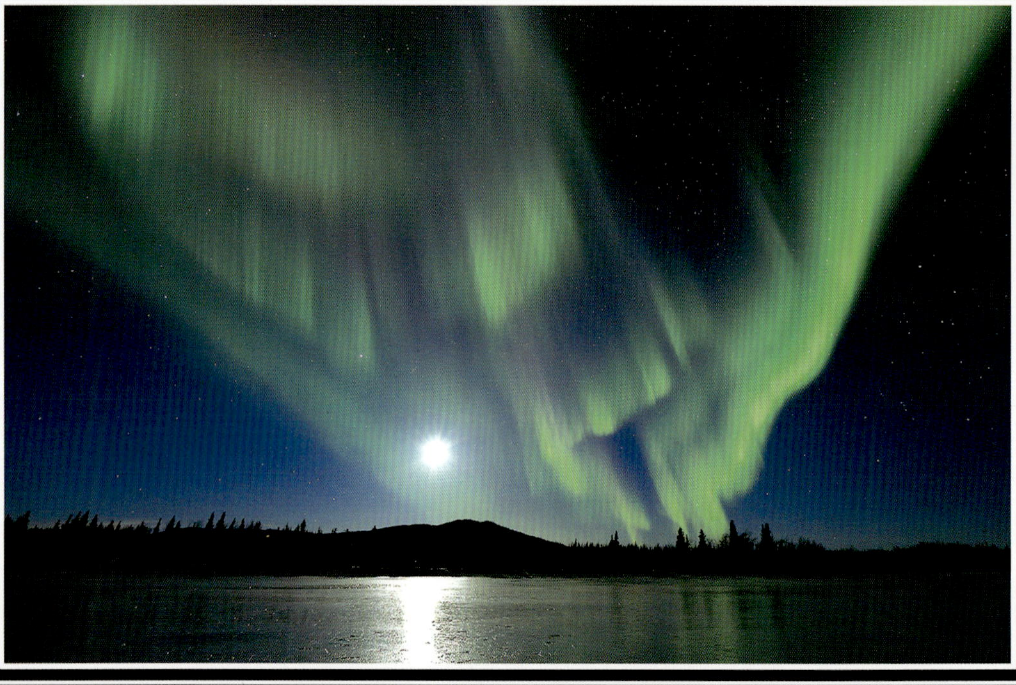

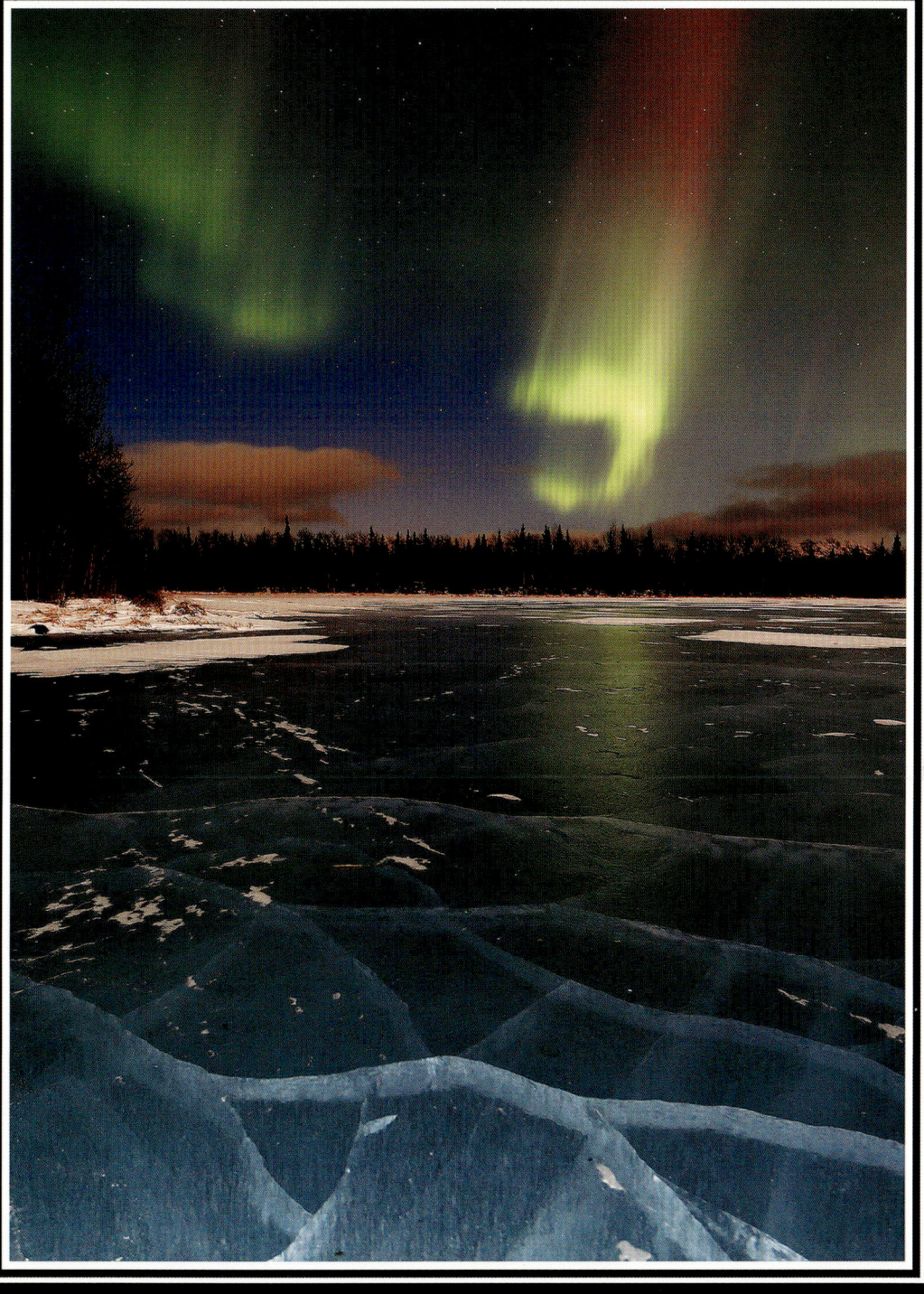

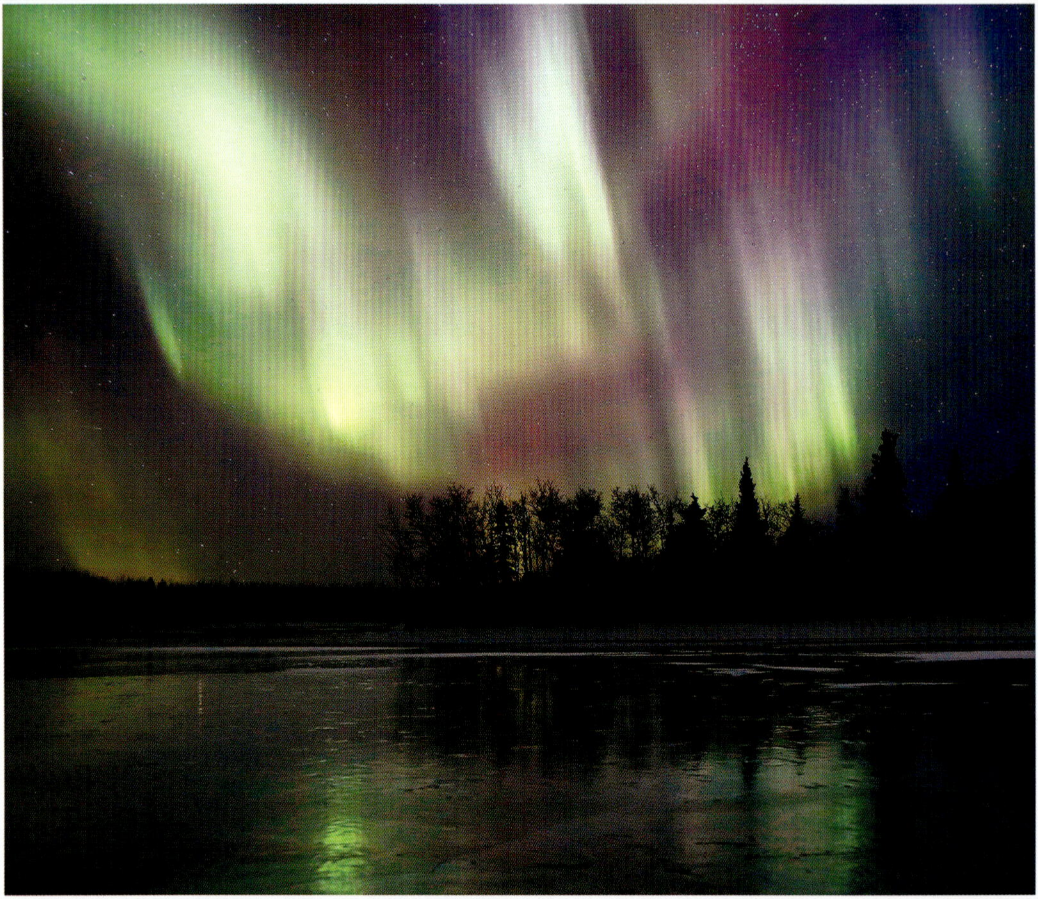

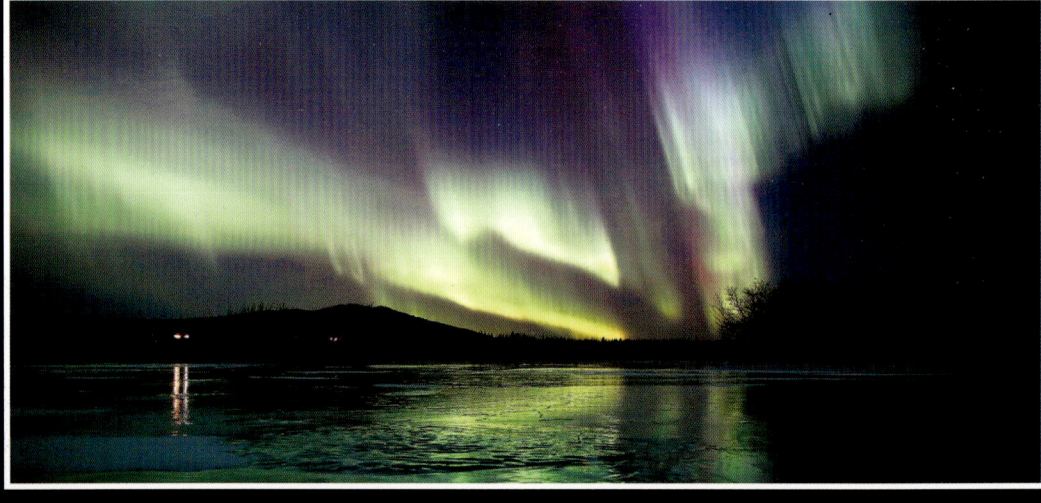

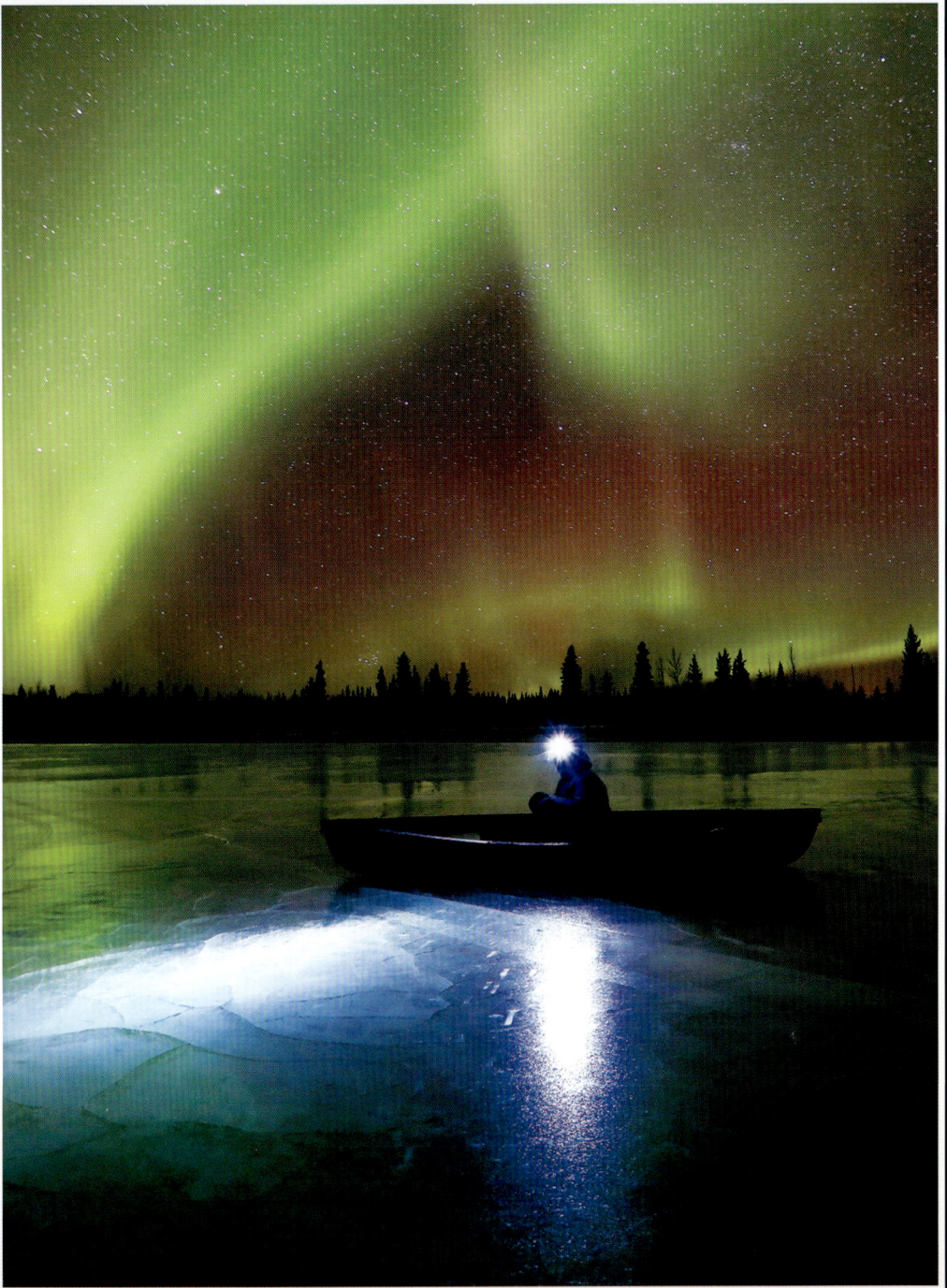

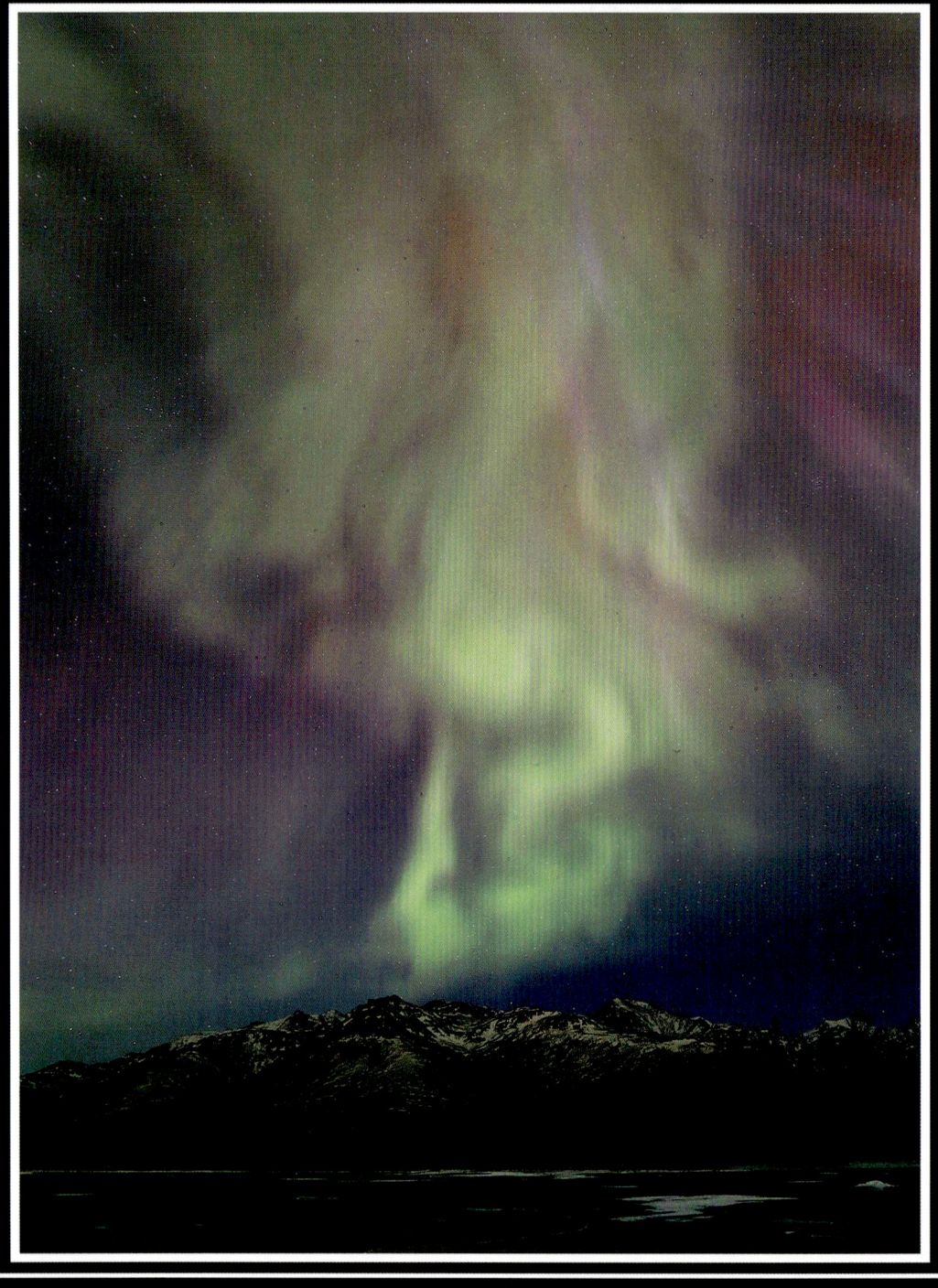

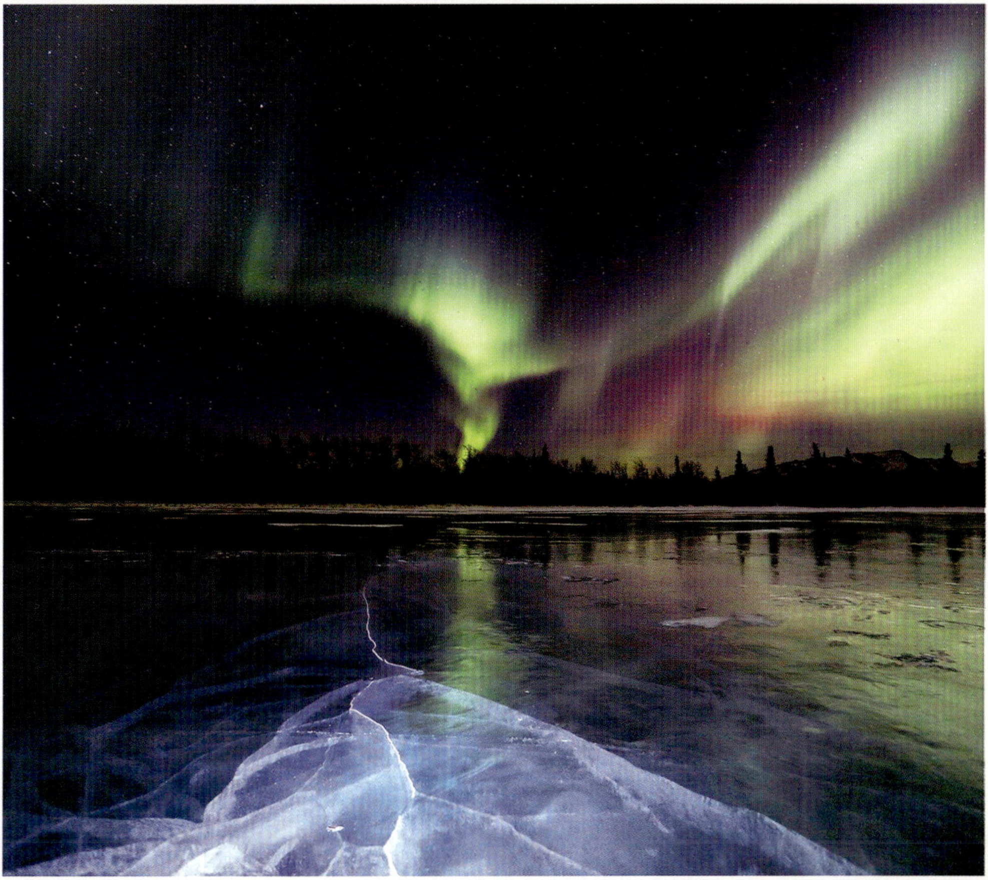

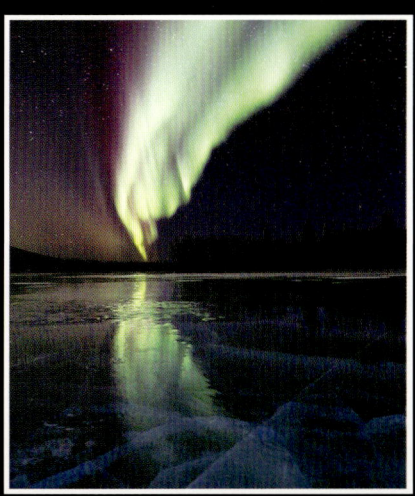
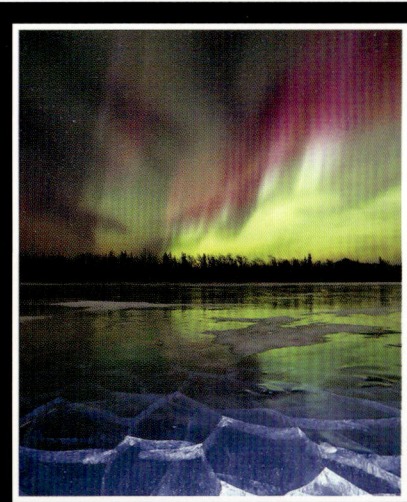

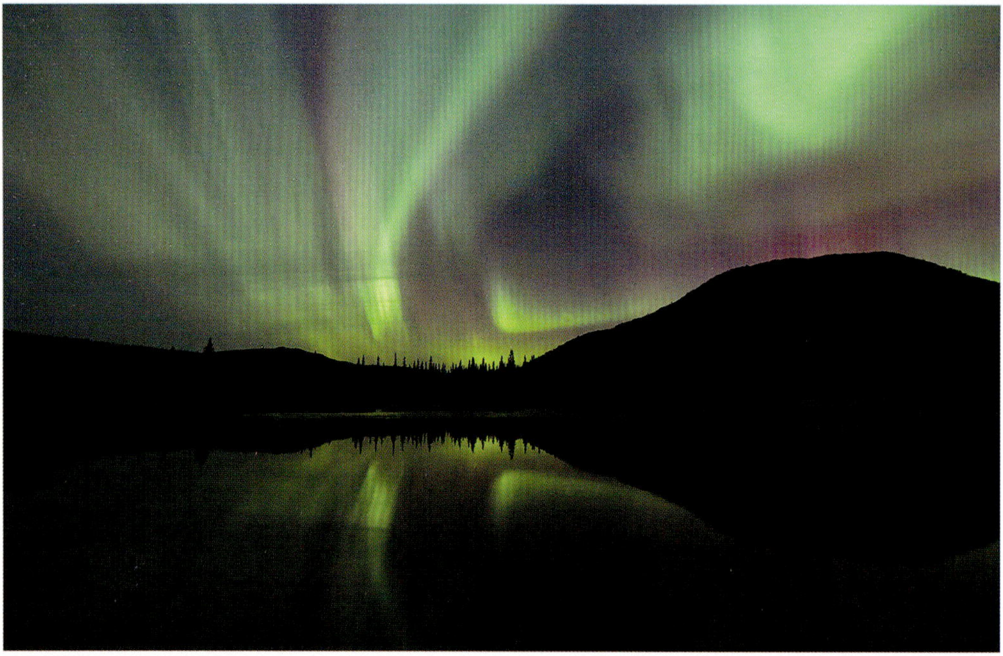

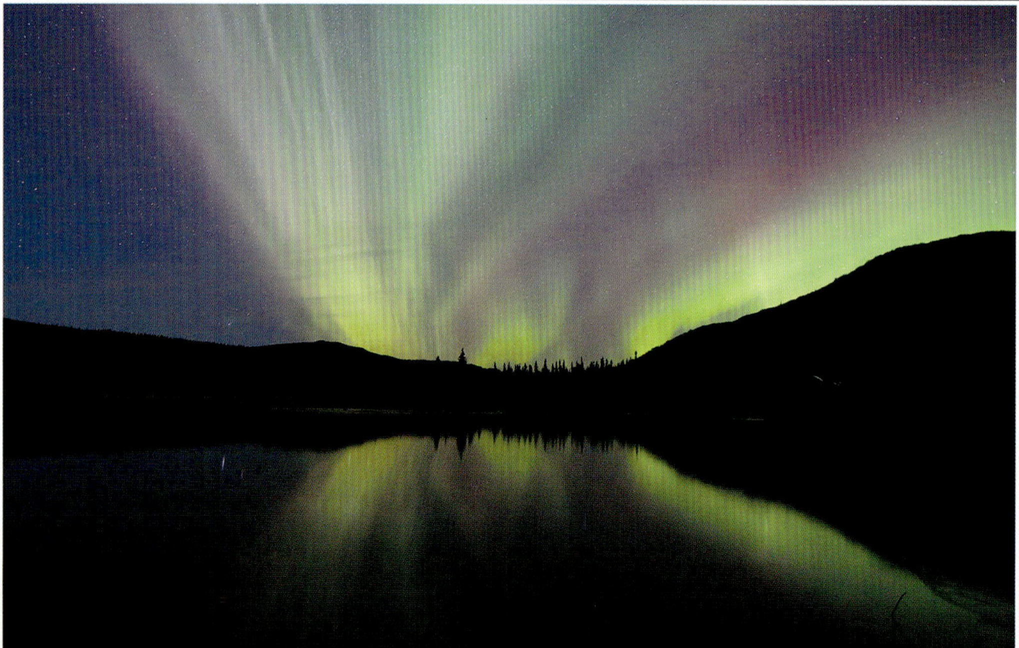

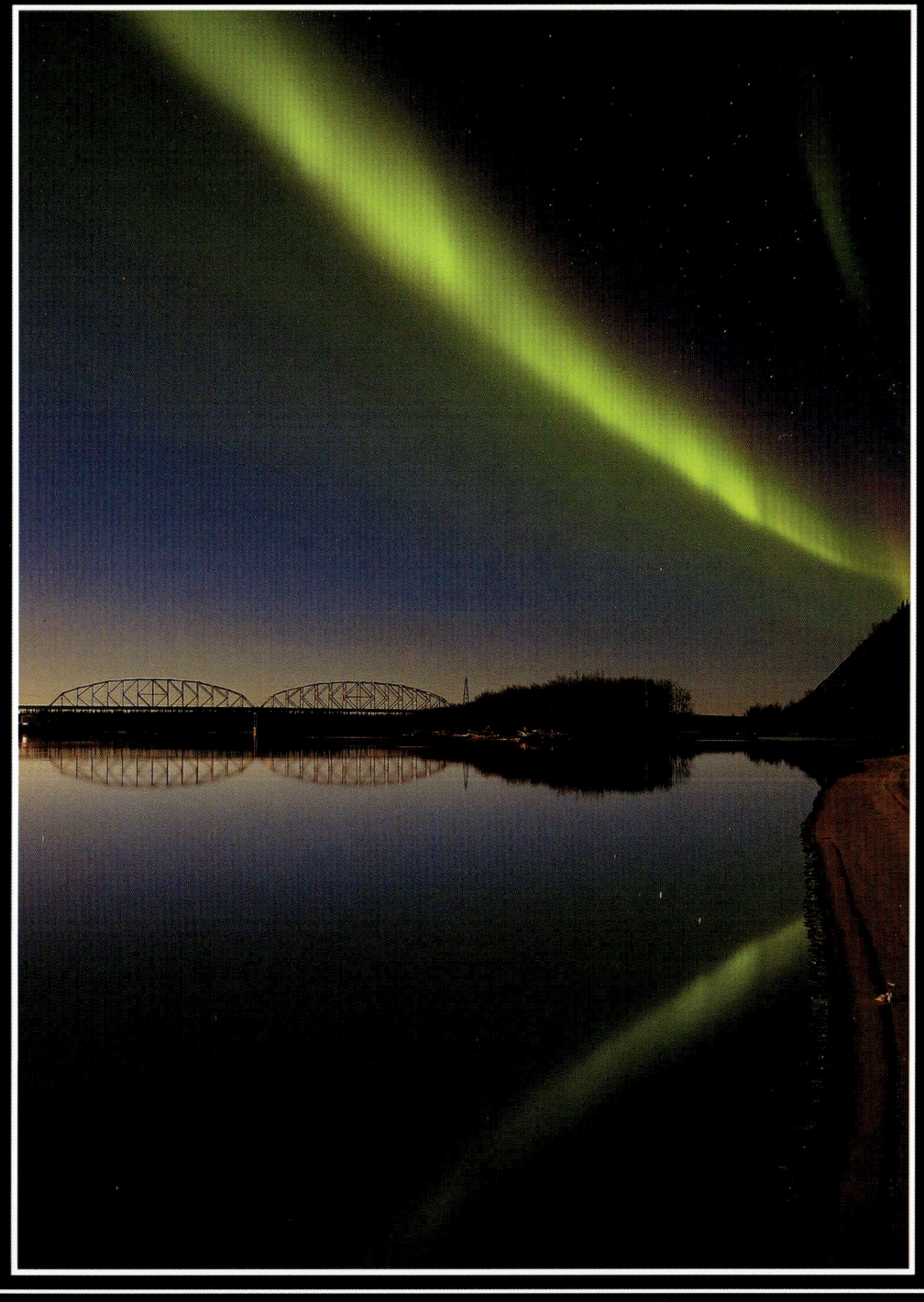

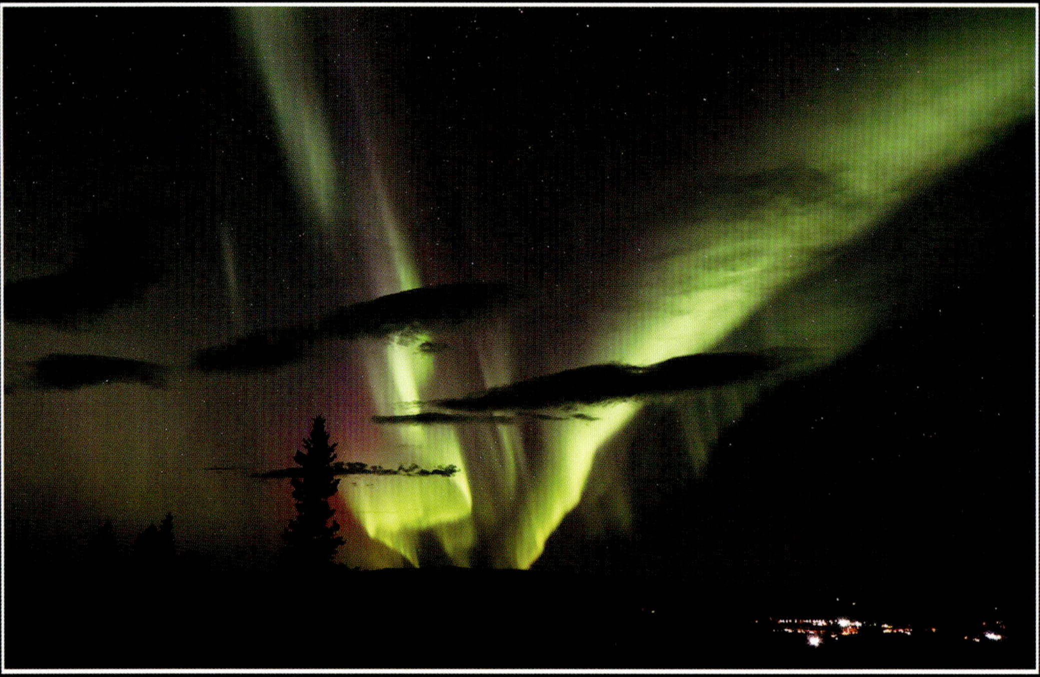

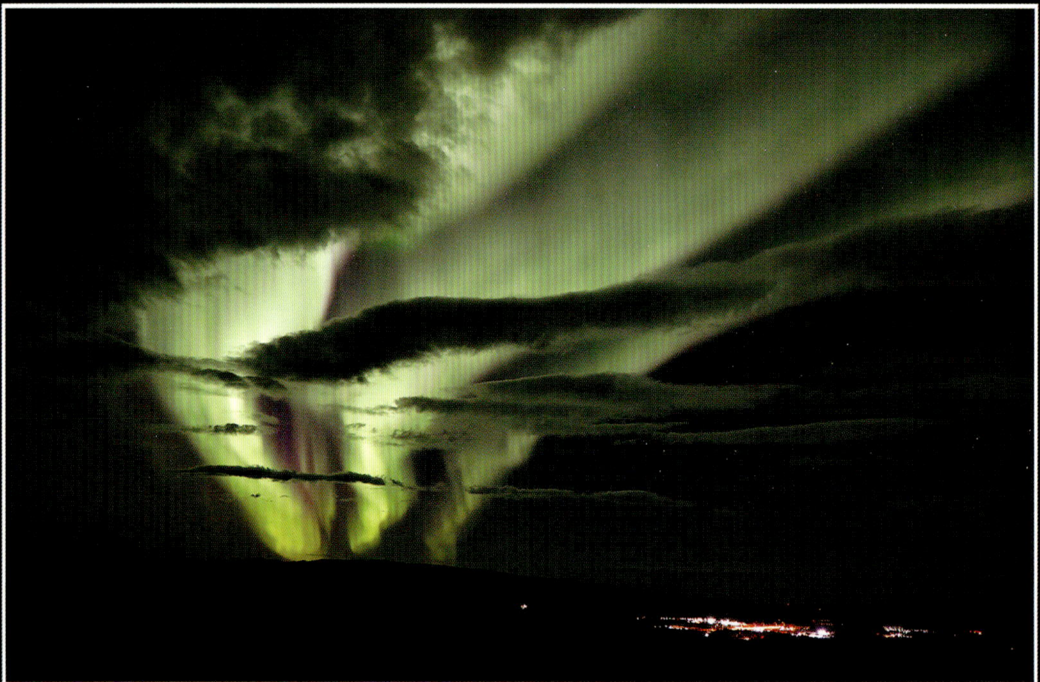

Precious Moments

As the thick clouds parted and the night sky cleared,
the view of endless stars suddenly reappeared.

In the shape of a backwards S was a shimmering light
that soon transformed the cold and dark, lonely night.

It had started out as a dull white, yellowish green
and quickly turned into a spectacular scene.

Green streaks were capped with purple and pink,
as the yellow crescent moon continued to sink.

It sunk past the horizon and down out of view,
as the light show unfolded, got brighter and grew.

The sound of wolves howling off in the distant hills
sent a shiver down my spine and filled my body with chills.

They were chills of delight knowing that this was unique.
Silence interrupted the primal sounds, I felt the mystique.

The sounds from the hills to the sights in the sky,
with the deep silence intermixed, I felt a natural high.

It was a high I had felt before from totally immersing in the now.
It was intense, yet pure and simple, it felt healthy, I yelled wow!

And the lights up above, they curtained and streaked,
as the ice on a nearby pond softly crackled and creaked.

The wolves yips and their howls echoed off in the distance
and the wondrous light show fizzled out in an instance.

Precious moments like these, they come and they go.
Feeling them deep in our hearts is a great way to grow.

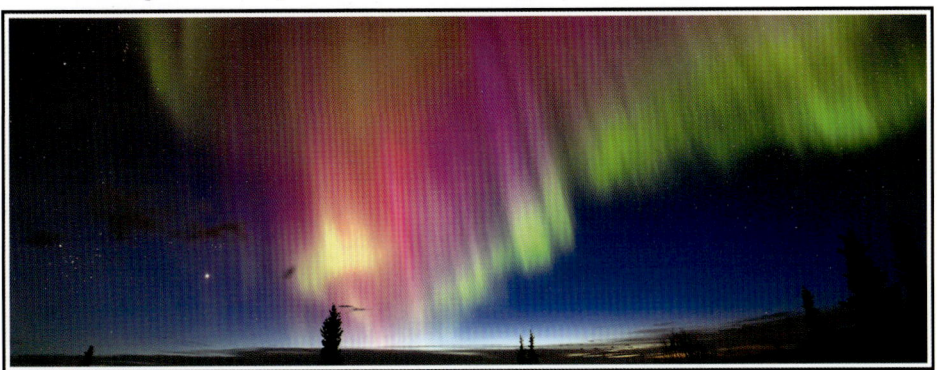

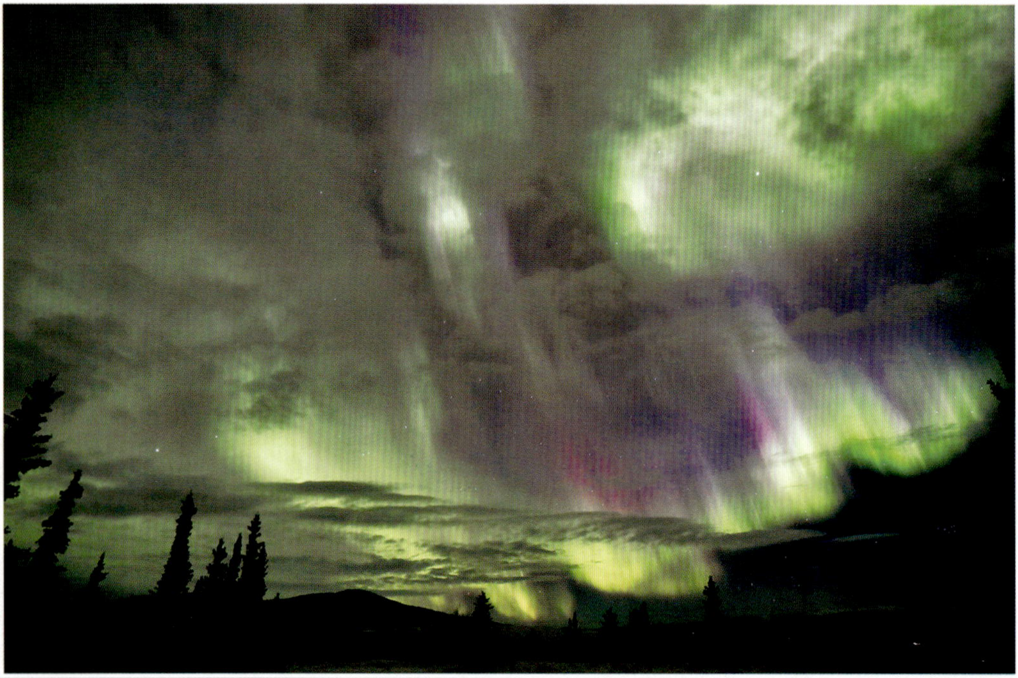

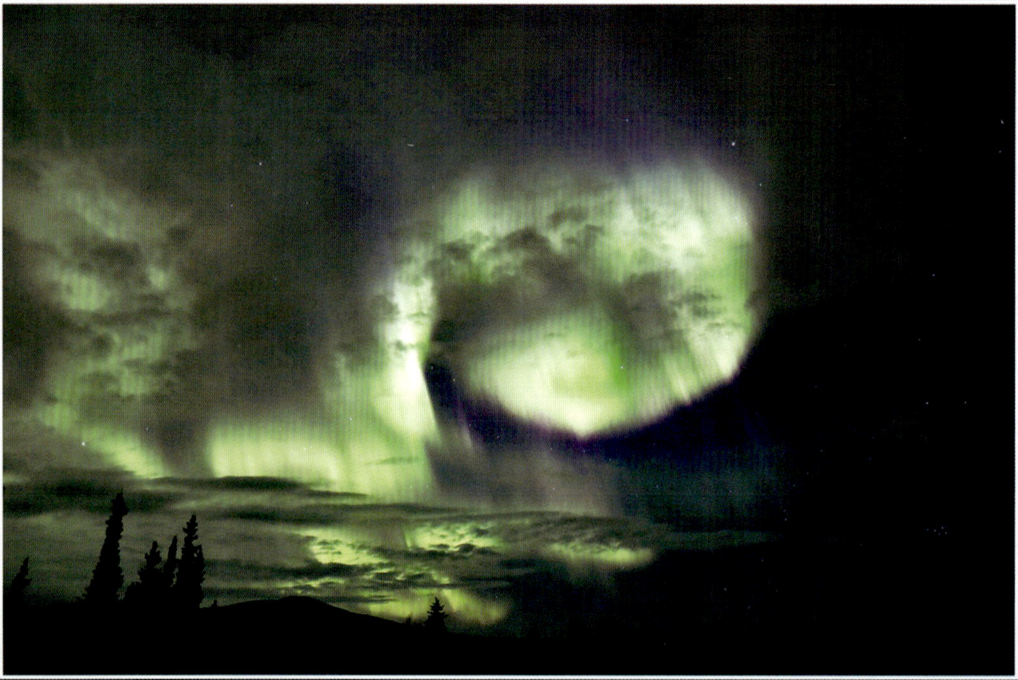

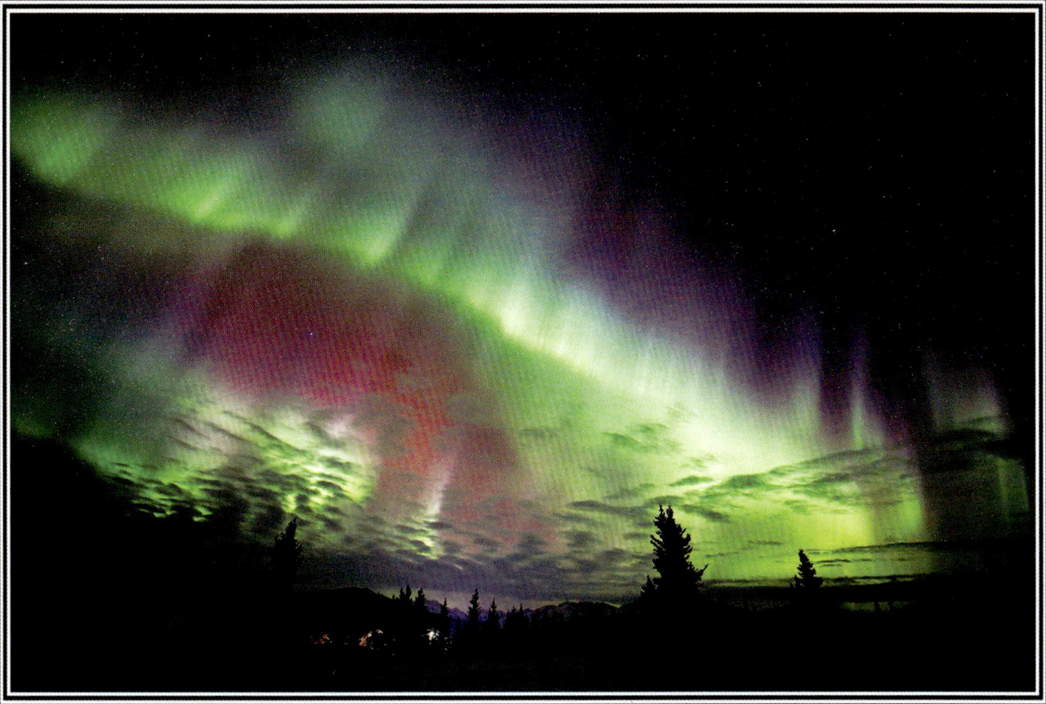

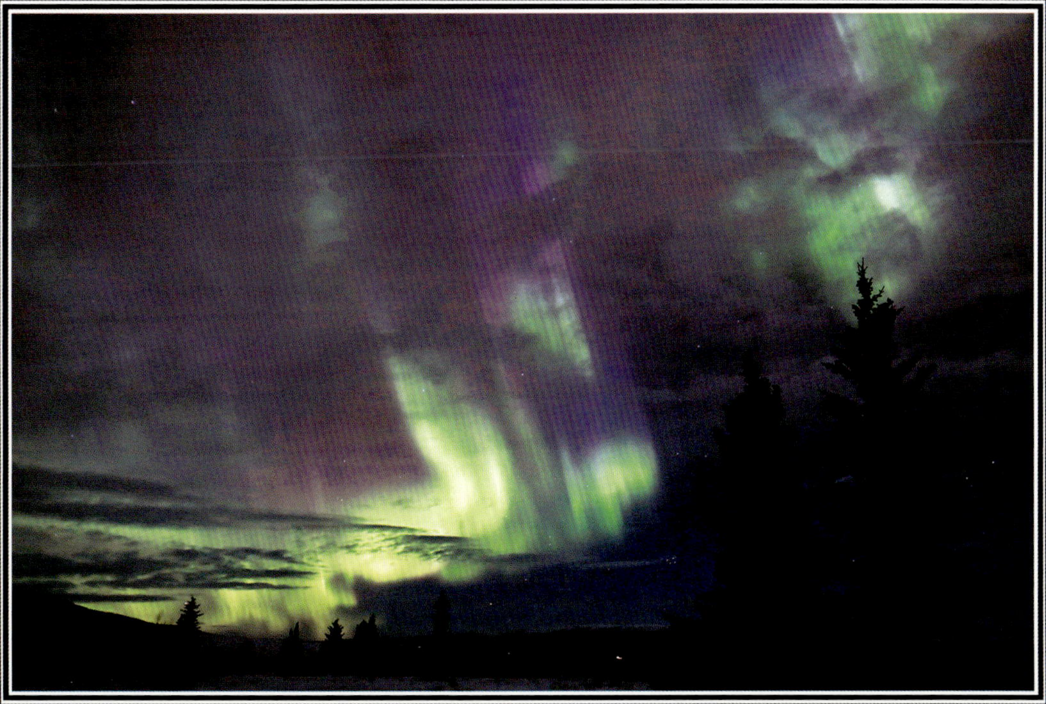

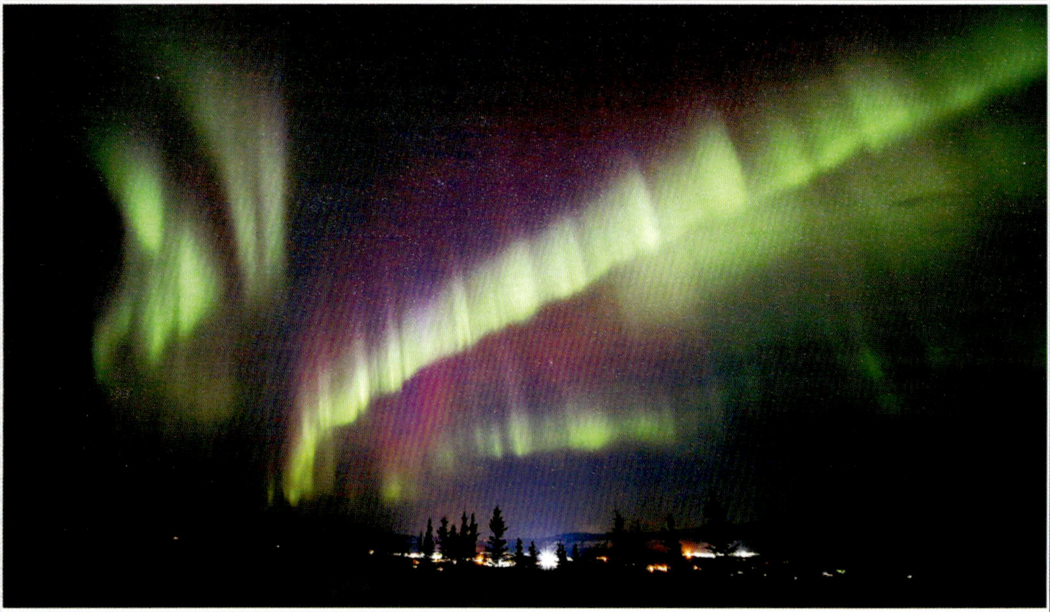

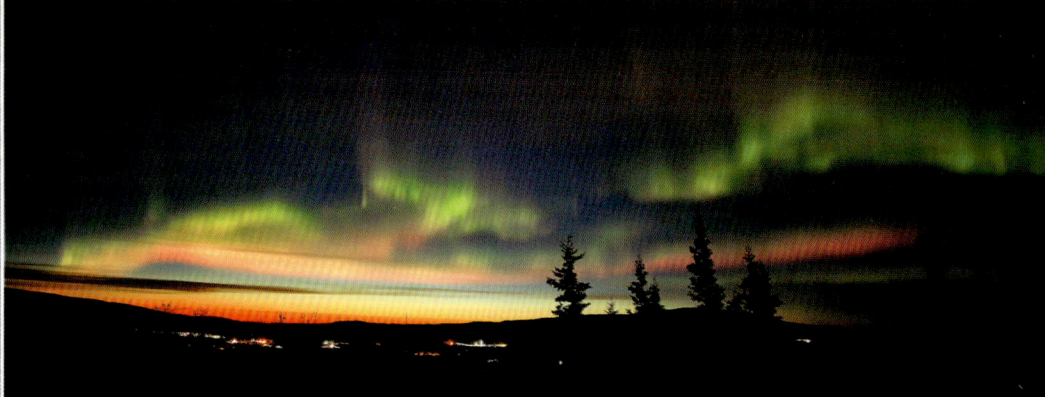
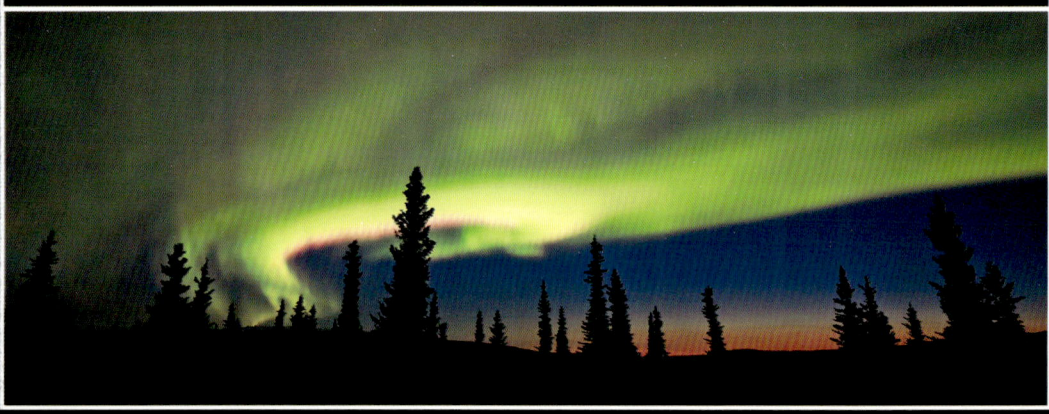

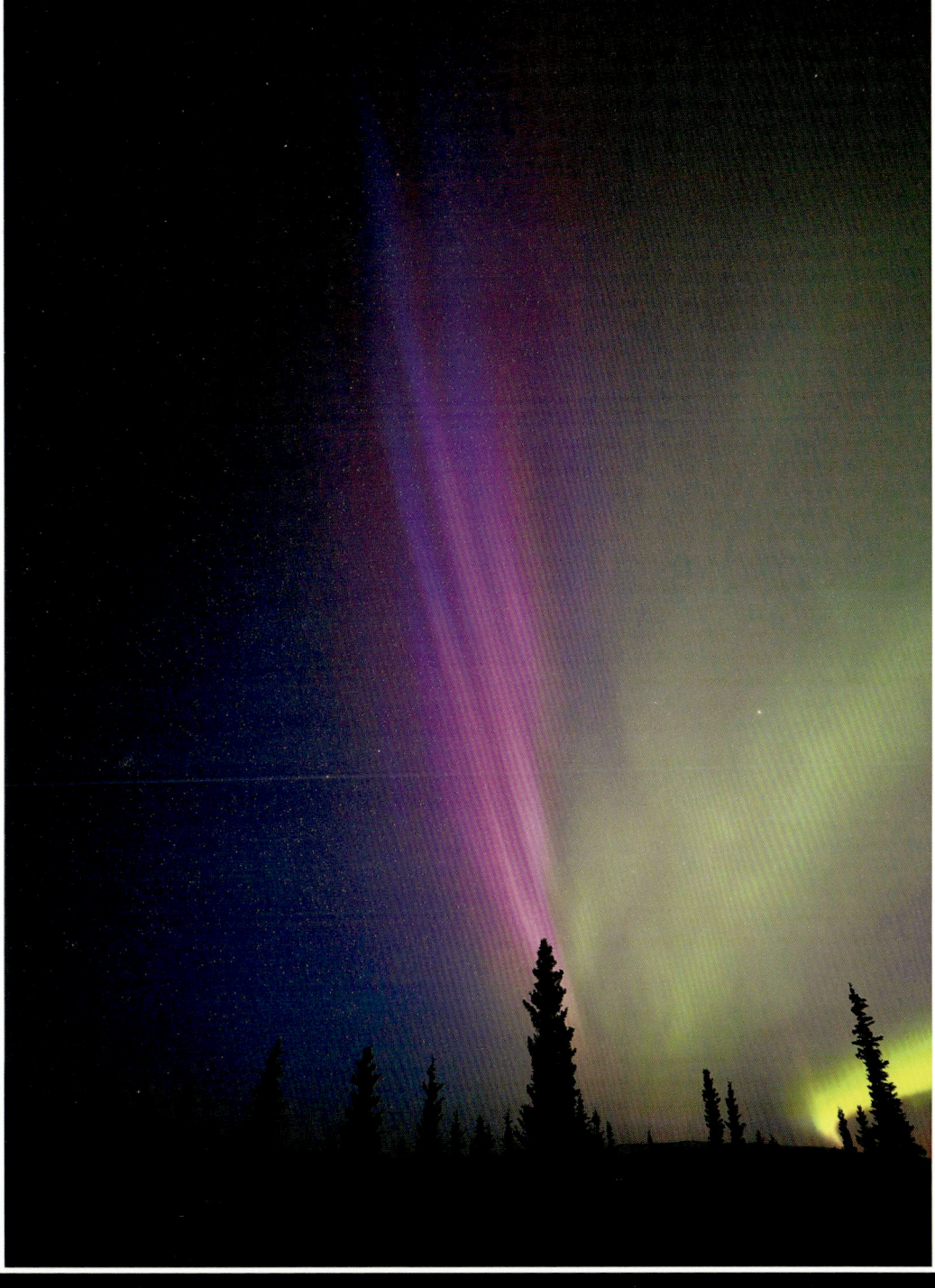

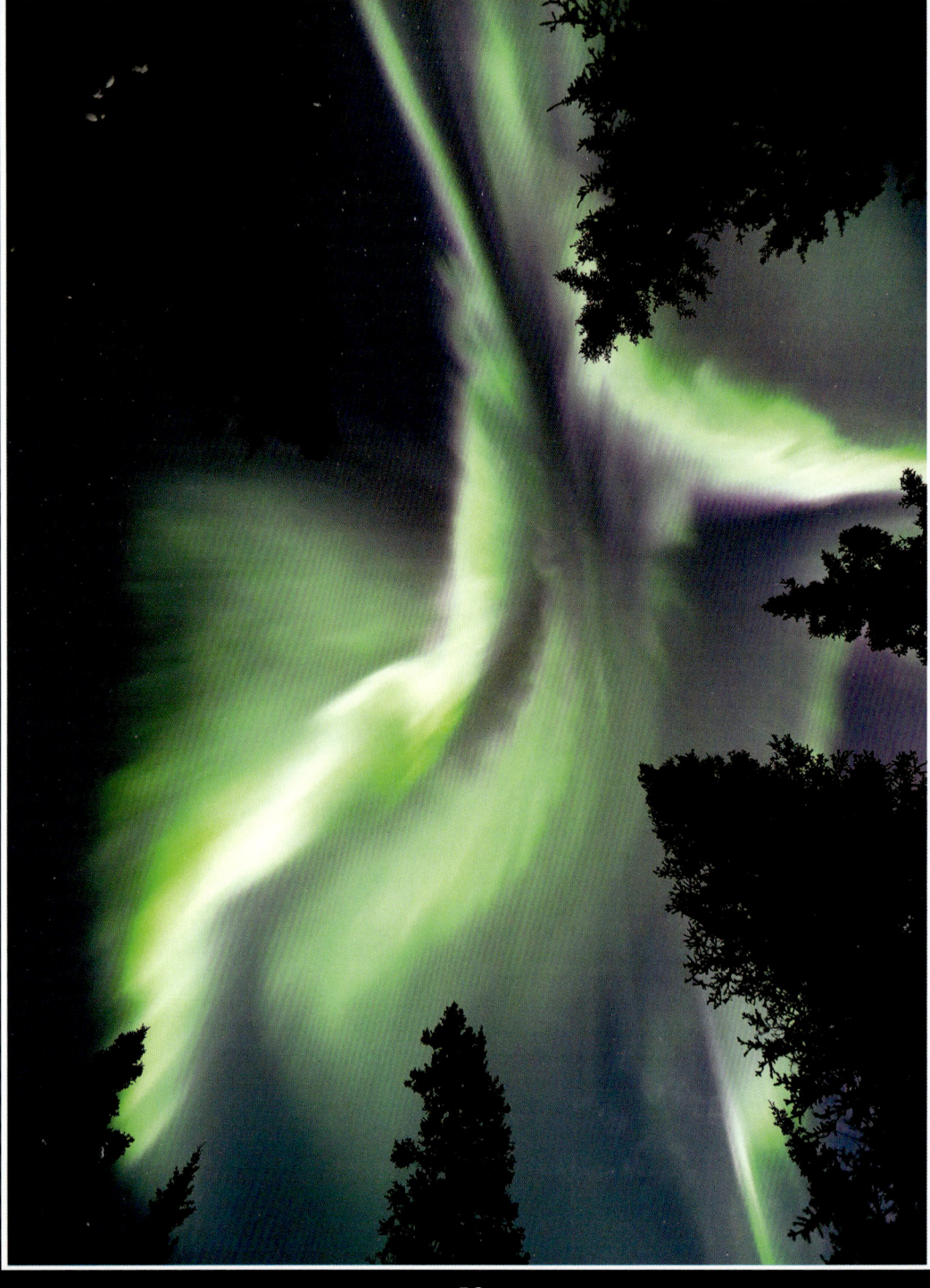

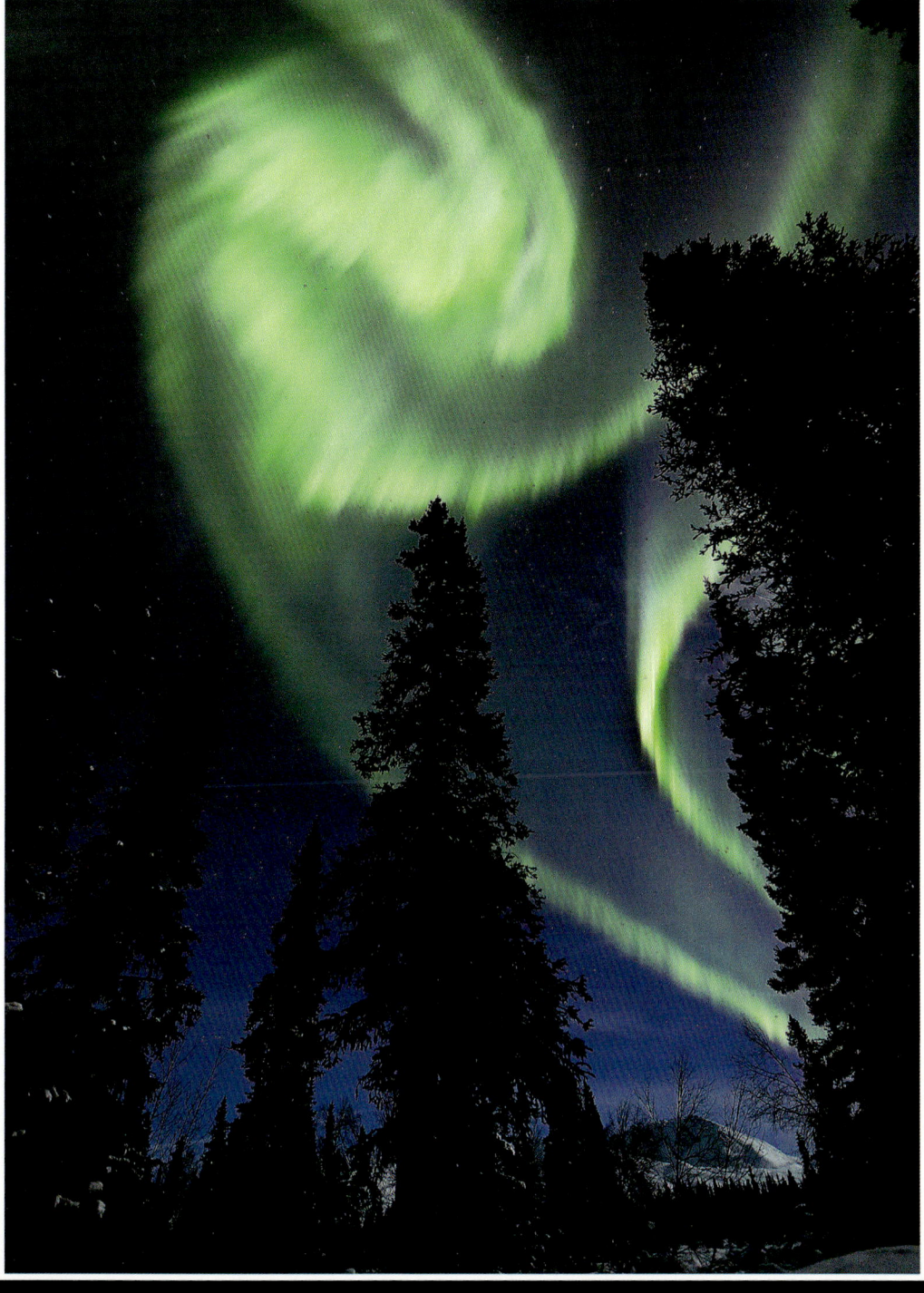

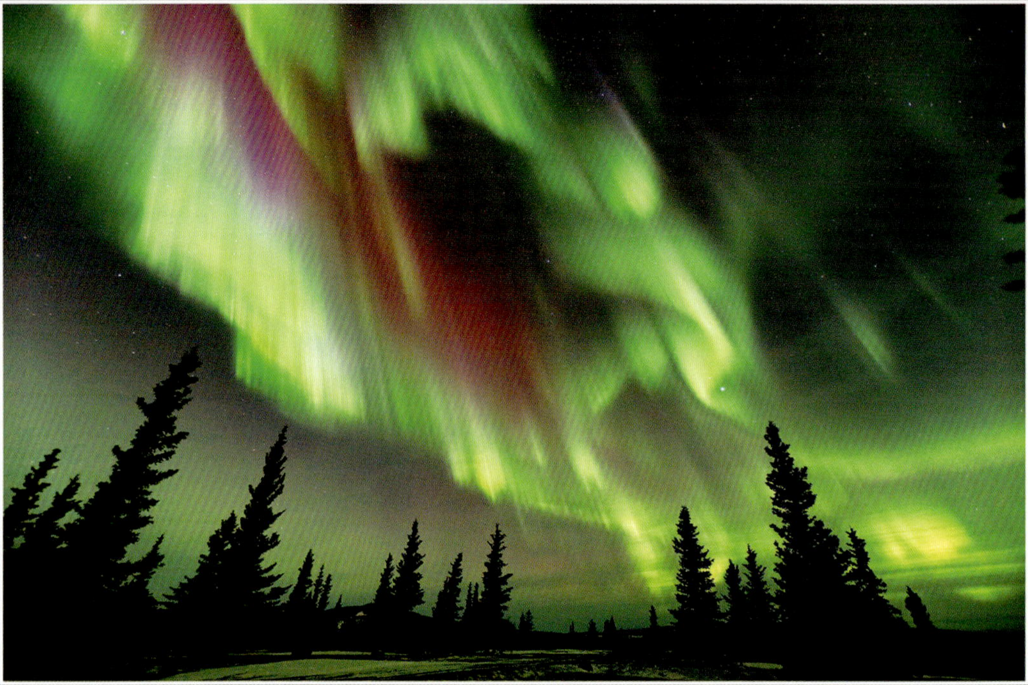

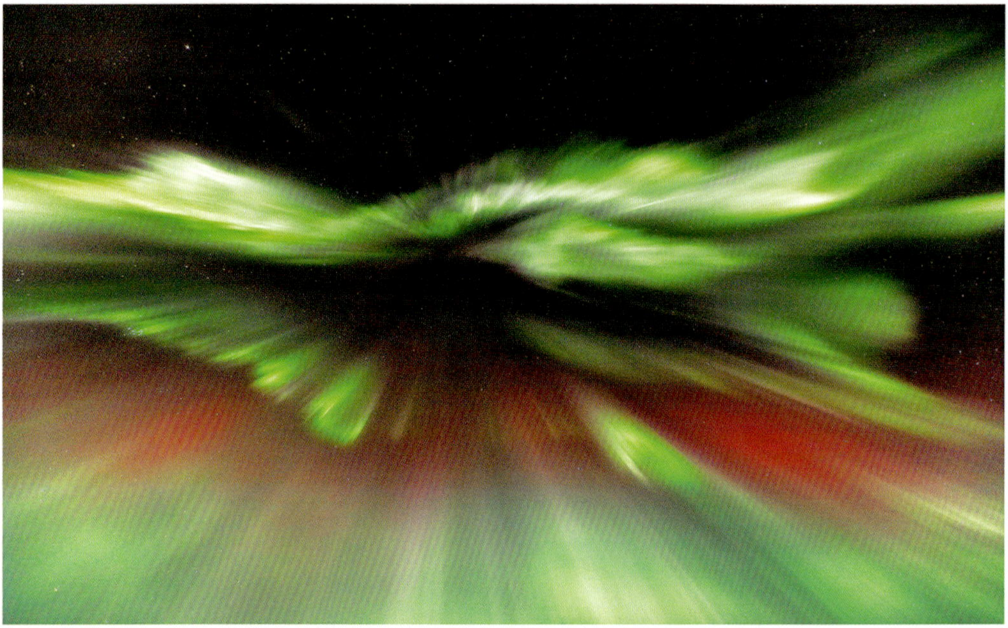

Colors Swirling in the Sky

The sky fills with colors
that swirl and curtain.
The wind stills
and silence creeps in.
Deep silence.
Healing silence.
A great horned owl
breaks the quiet
with a whoo whoo who whooo.
Explosions of red and green
straight overhead,
like an angel's wings
flapping in technicolor brilliance.
Whoo whoo who whooo.
An auroral corona
appears as a dog,
a ghost,
a fire breathing black hole;
completely changing
in an instant,
fizzling into curtains
dancing and draping
across the night sky.
Pink, purple, green and yellow
down to the horizon.
A lonely gust of air
interrupts the silence.
The deep silence.
The healing silence.
Whoo whoo who whooo.
The swirling curtains of color
move overhead,
again,
and explode,
again,
back into a corona.

Colors Swirling in the Sky

Flashing,
flaring,
pulsating rays
of color.
Whoo whoo who whooo.
And the deep silence returns
as the intensity of color
begins to fade
and fade
until the colors
swirling in the sky
surrender
back to the stars,
the planets
and the never ending blue-black.
Whoo whoo who whooo.
Oh, the sweet northern sky.

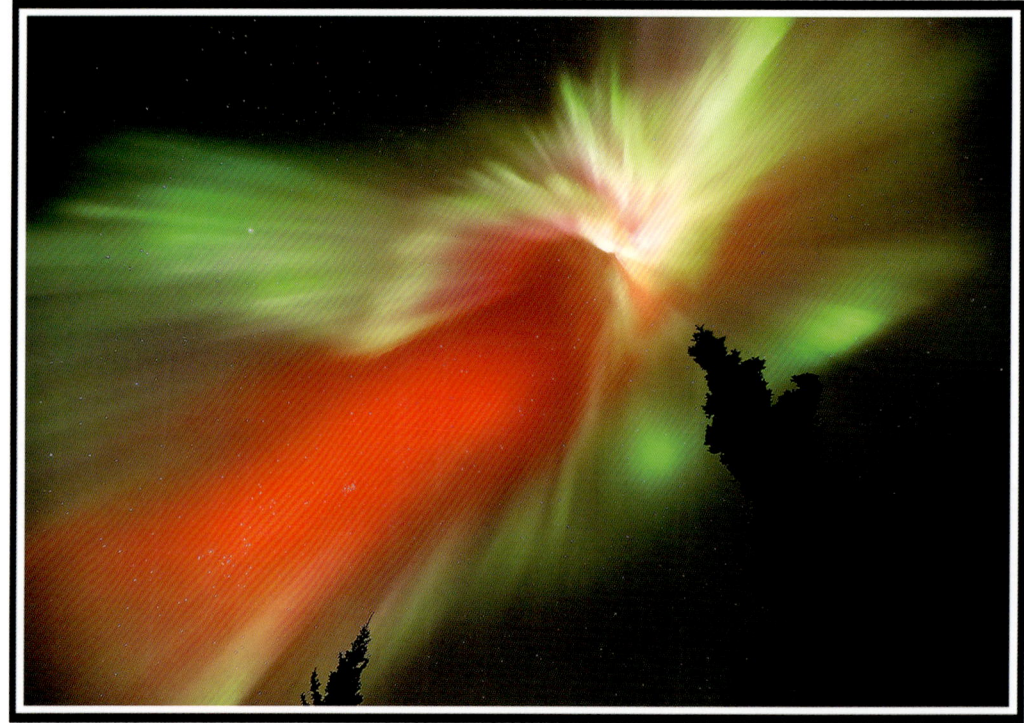

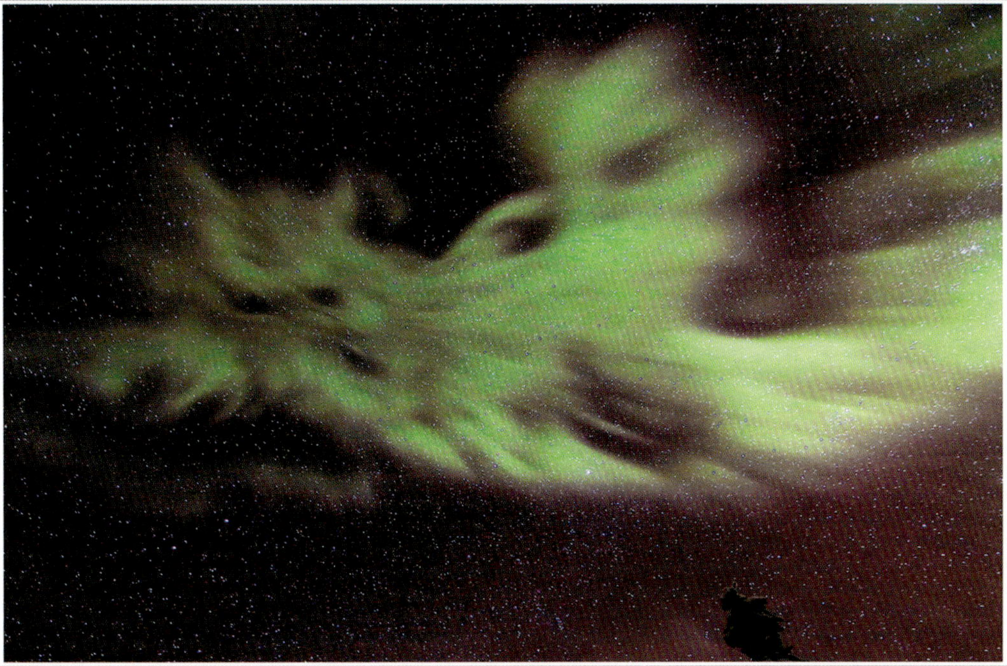

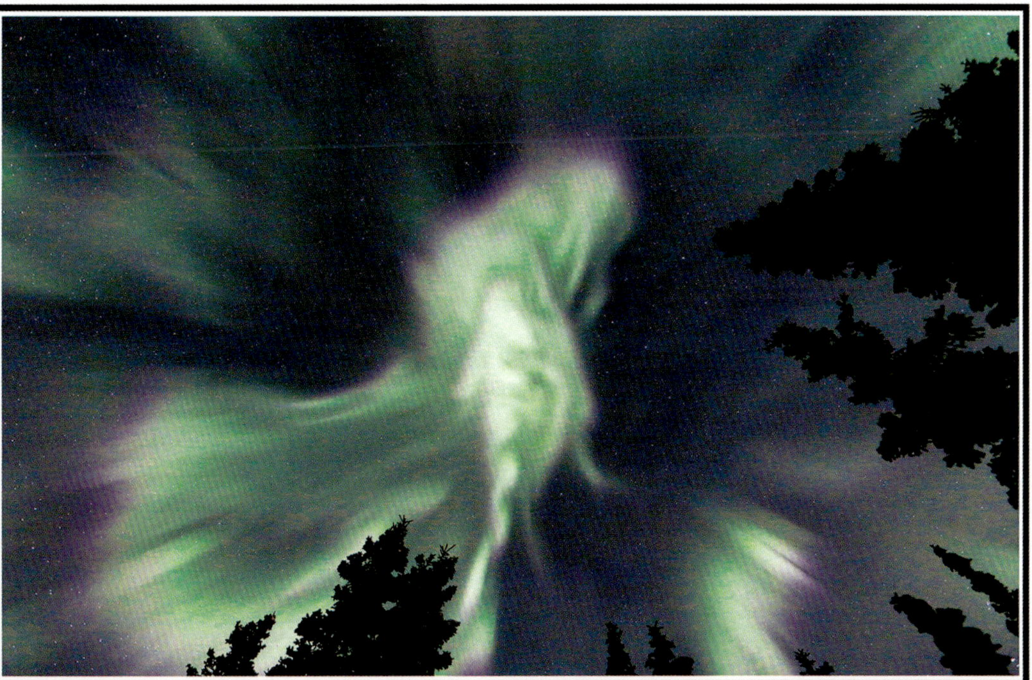

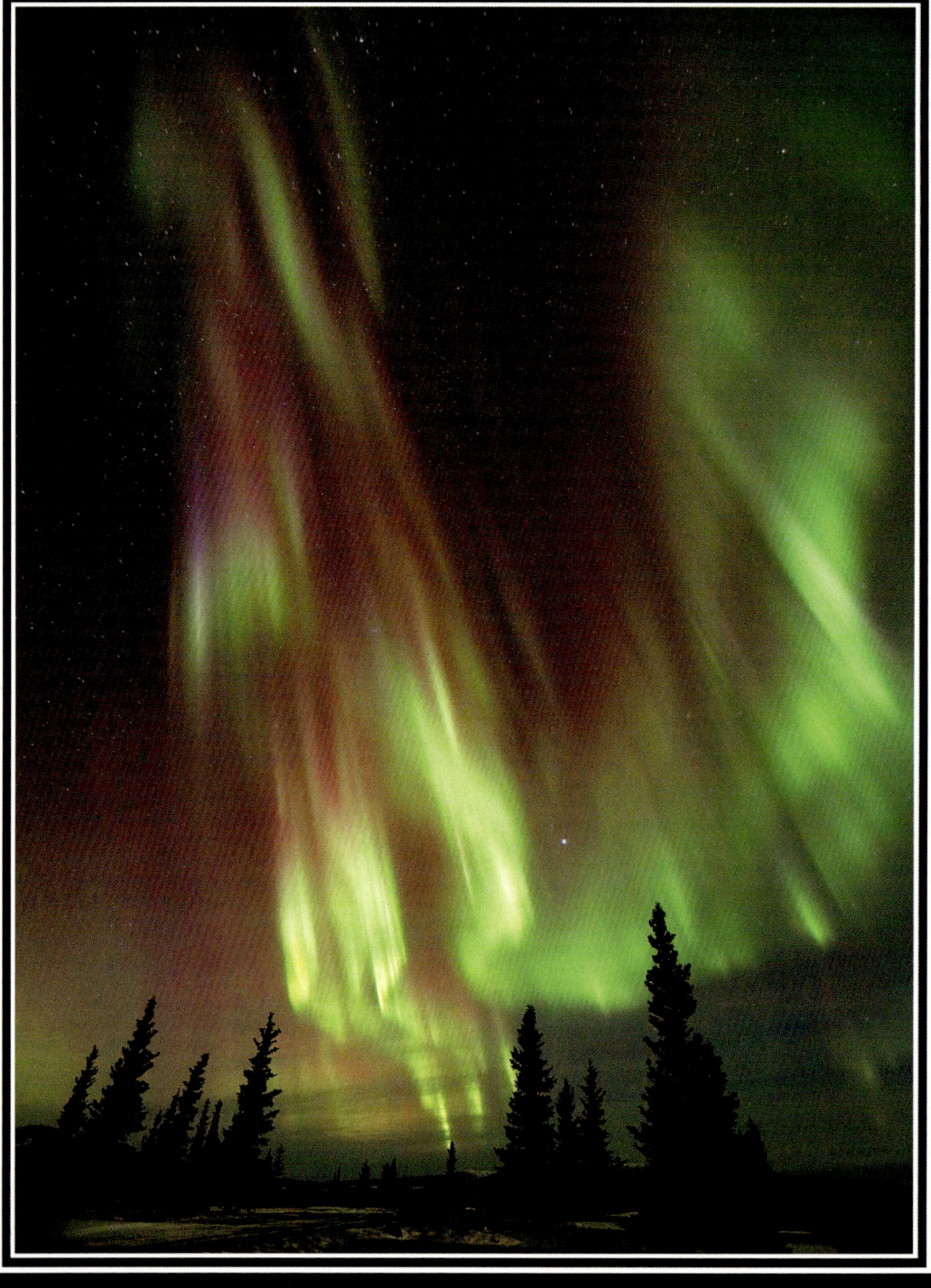

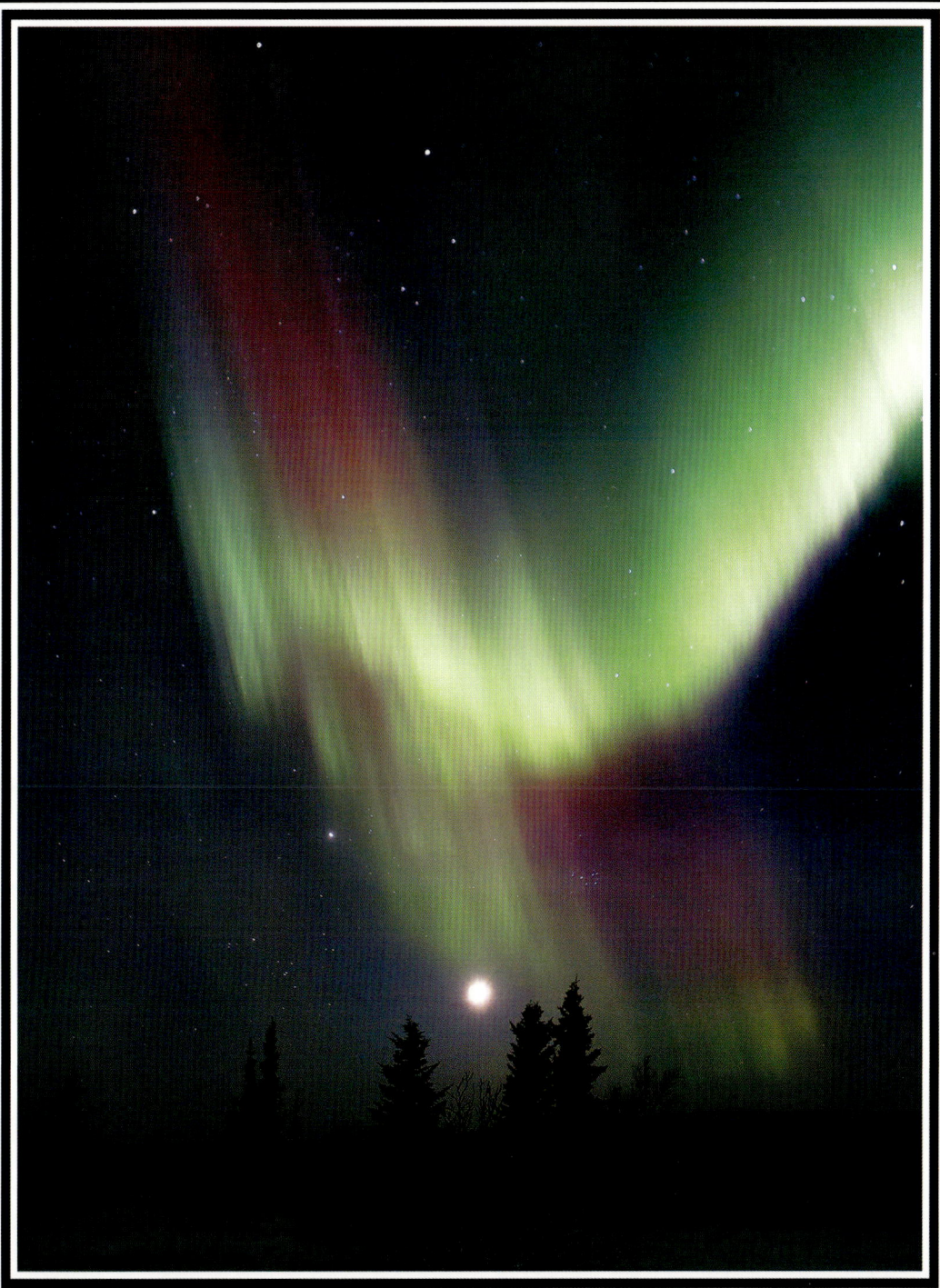

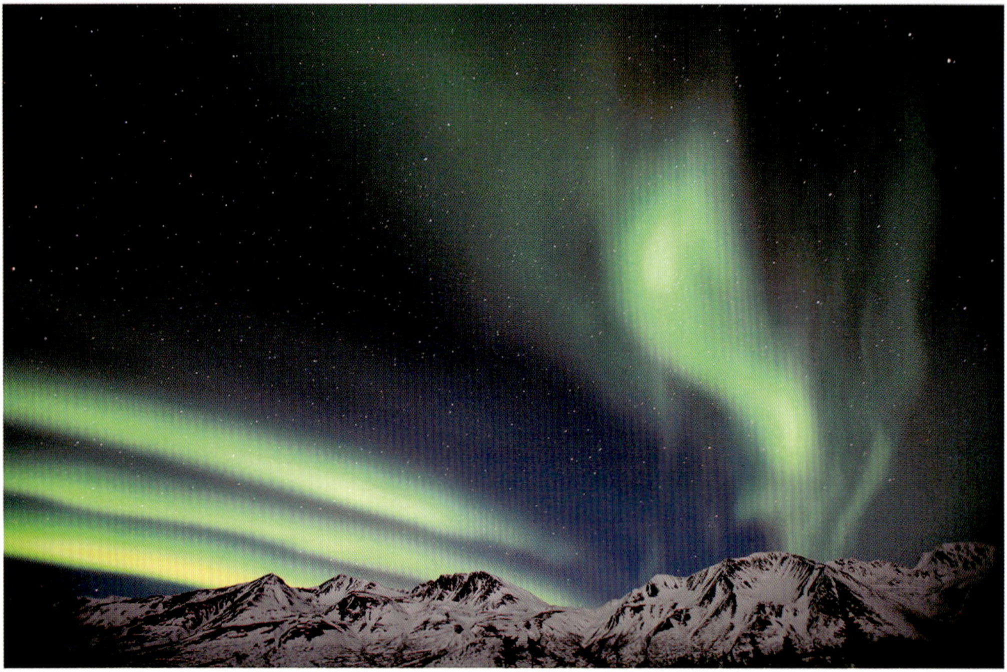

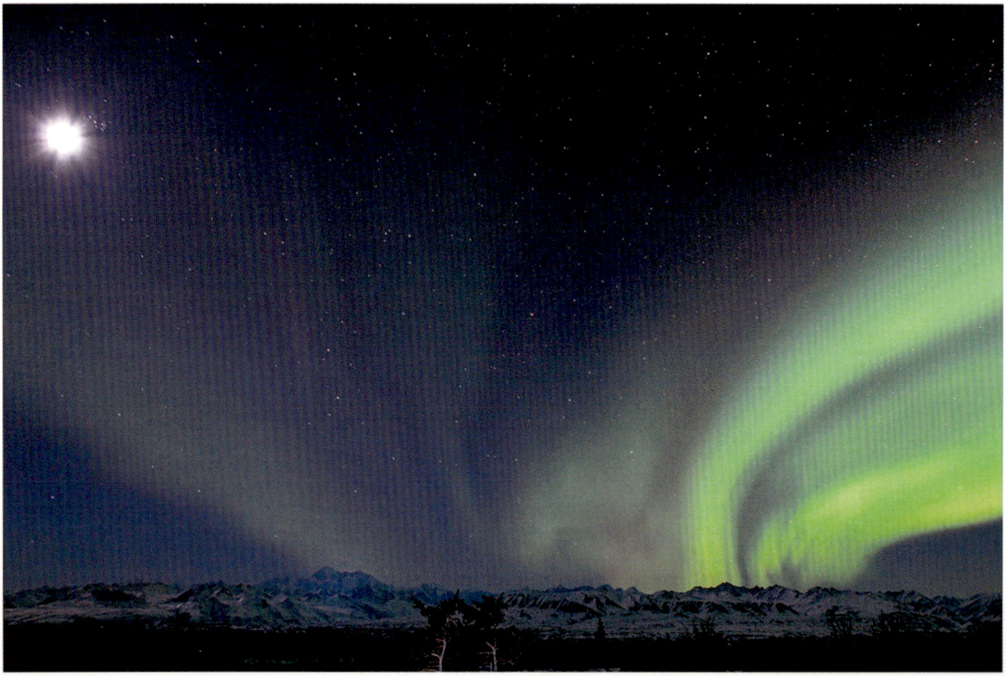

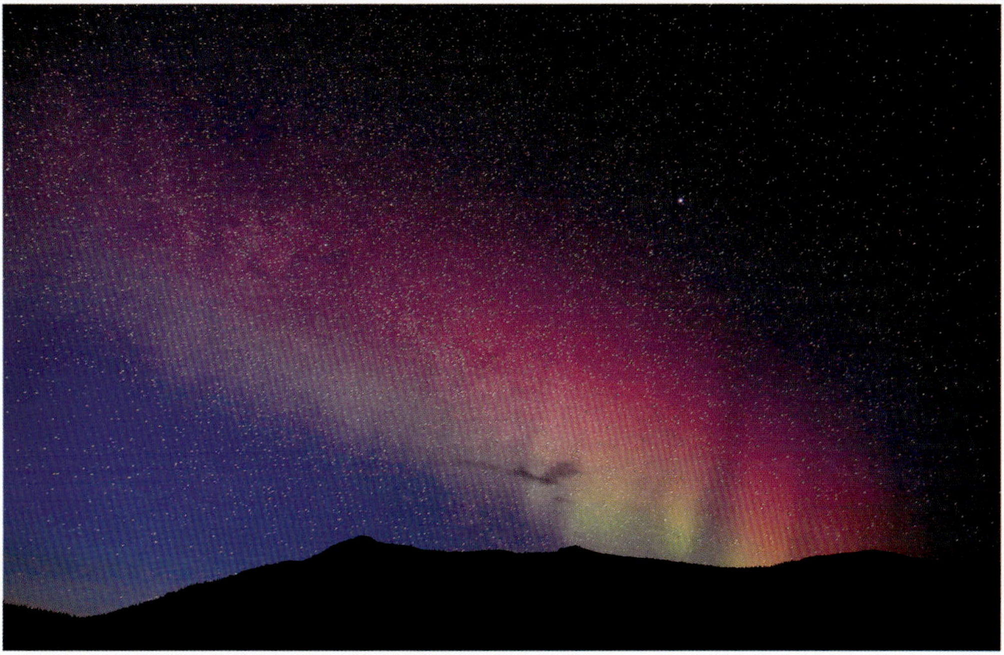

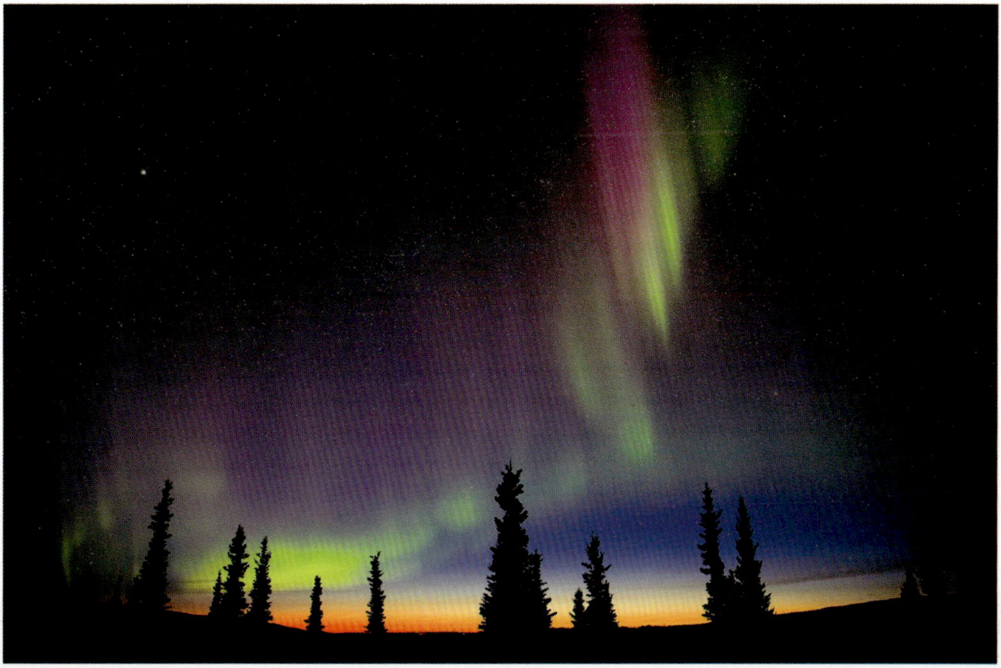

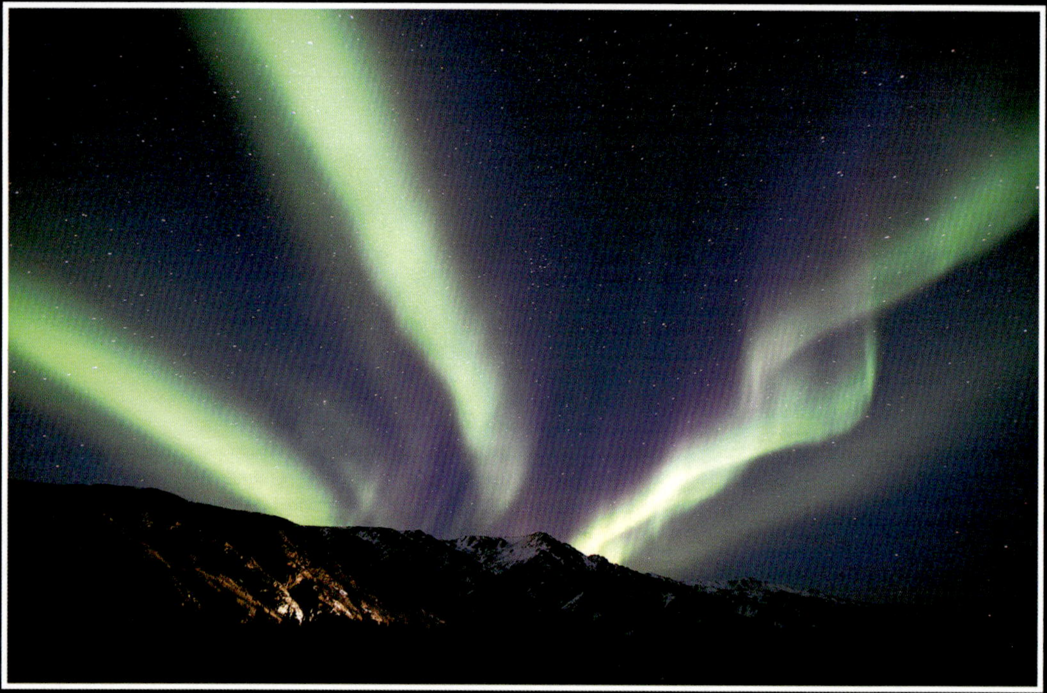

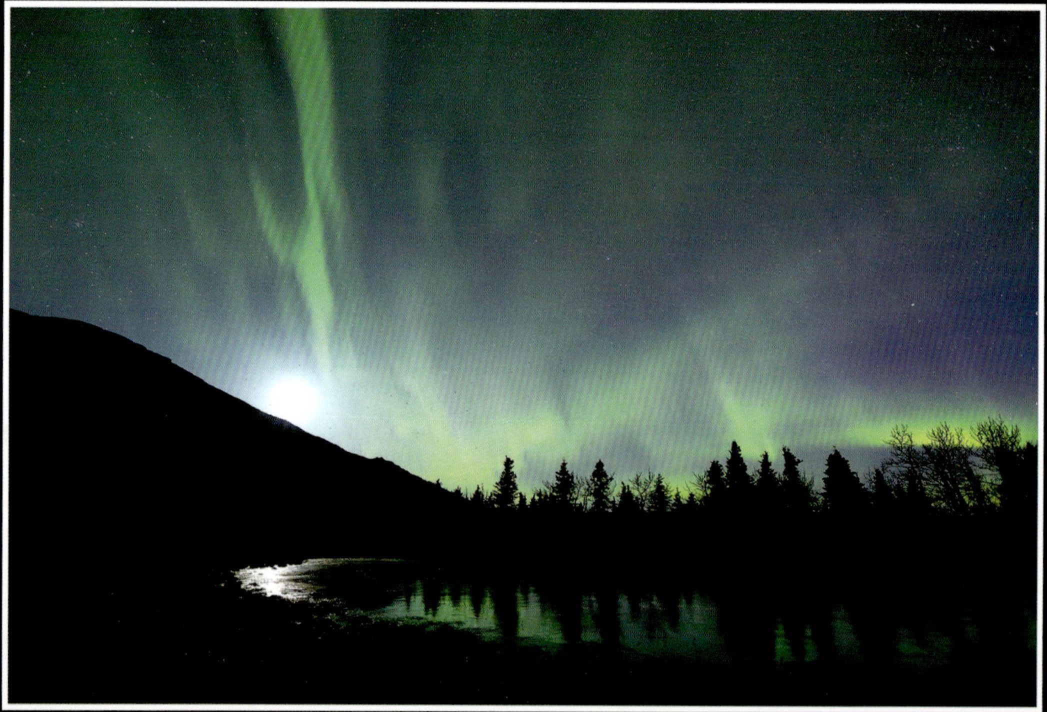

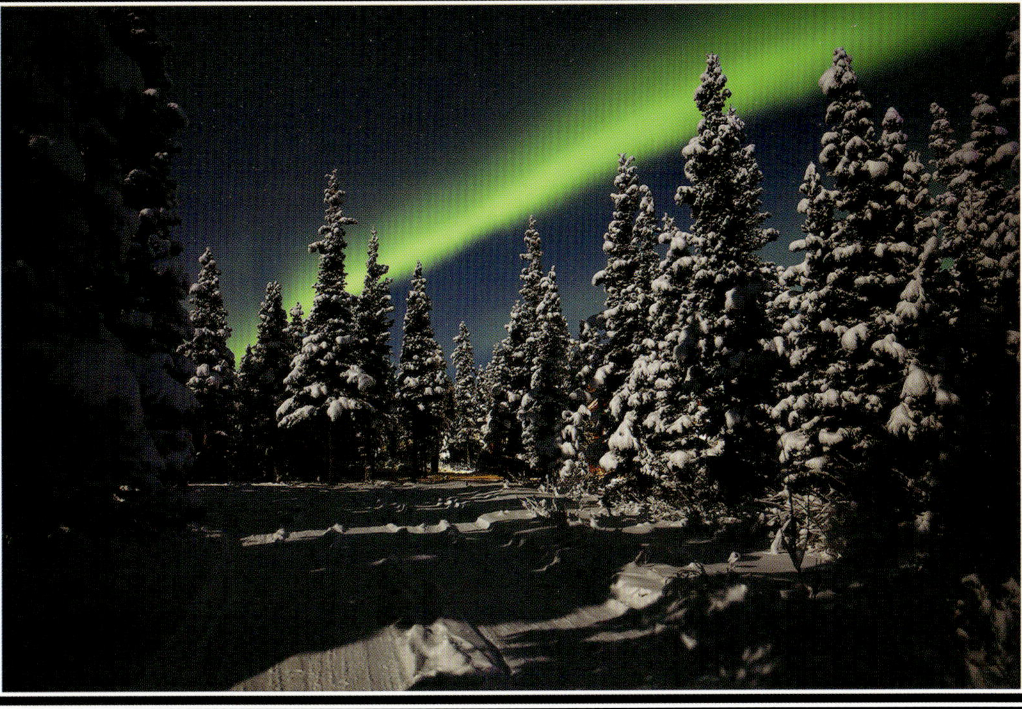

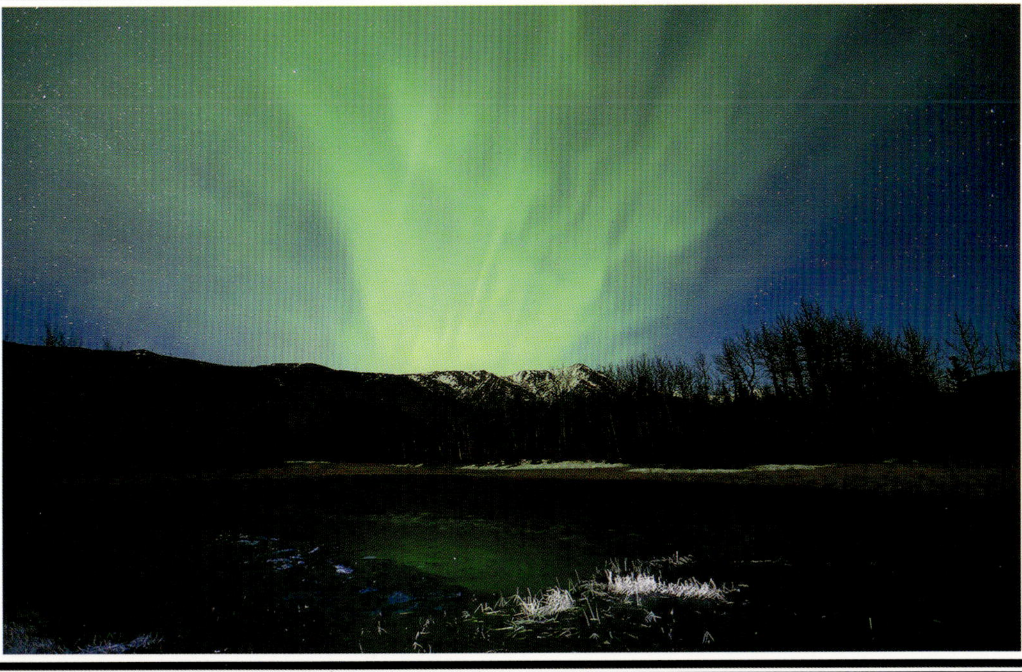

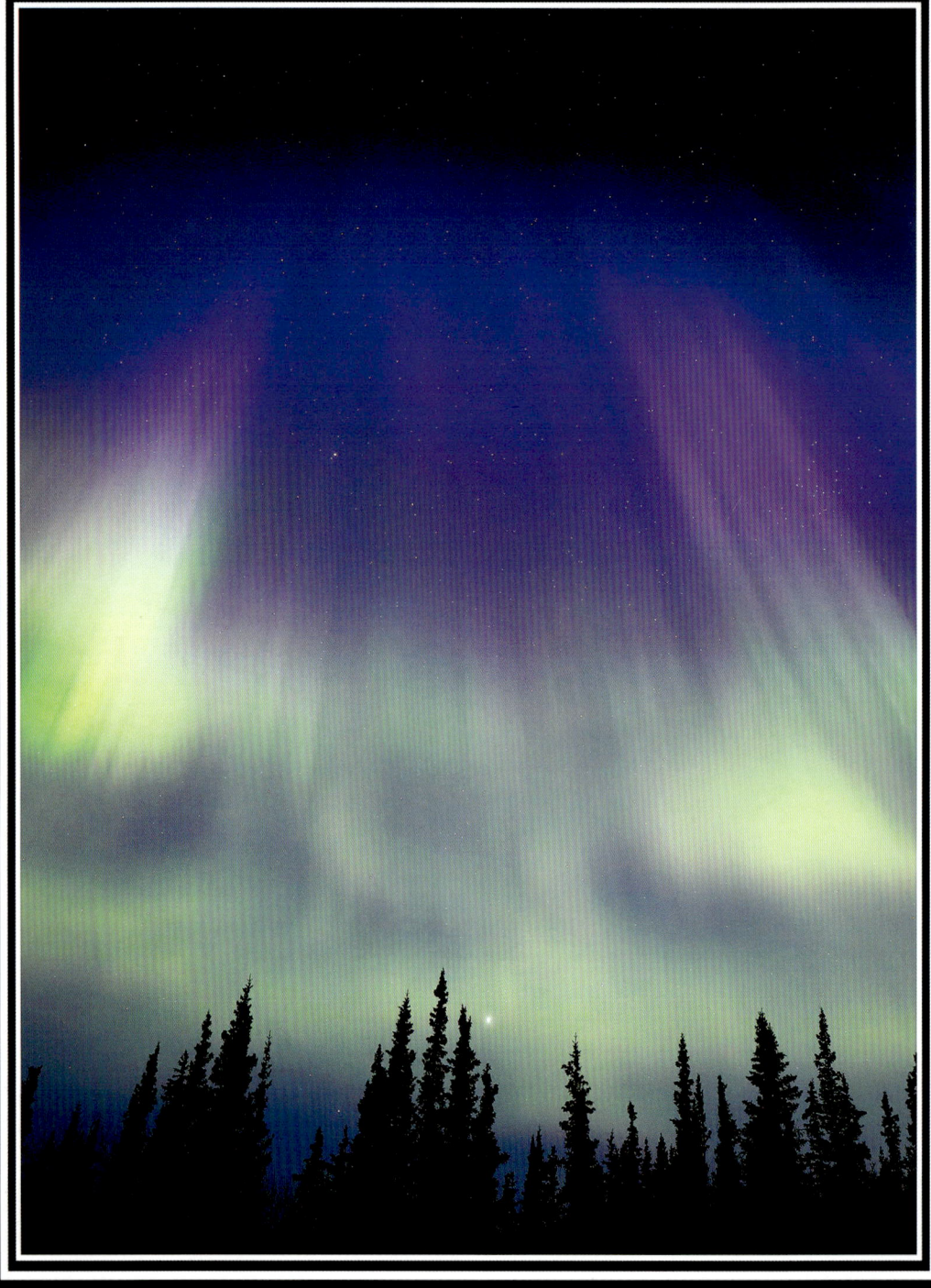

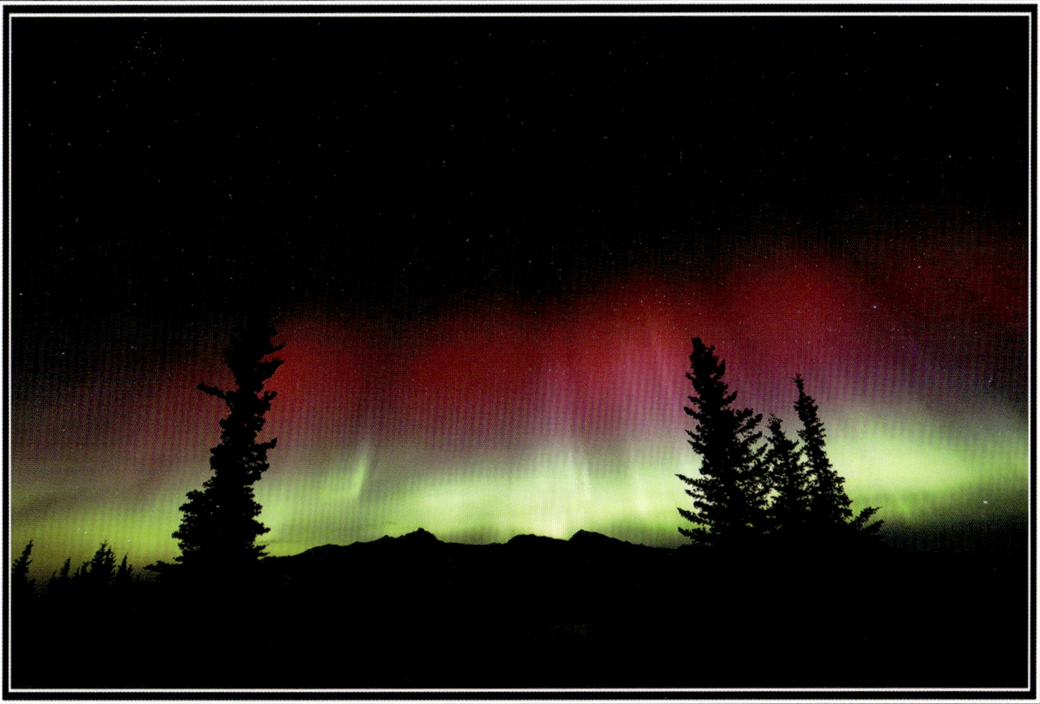

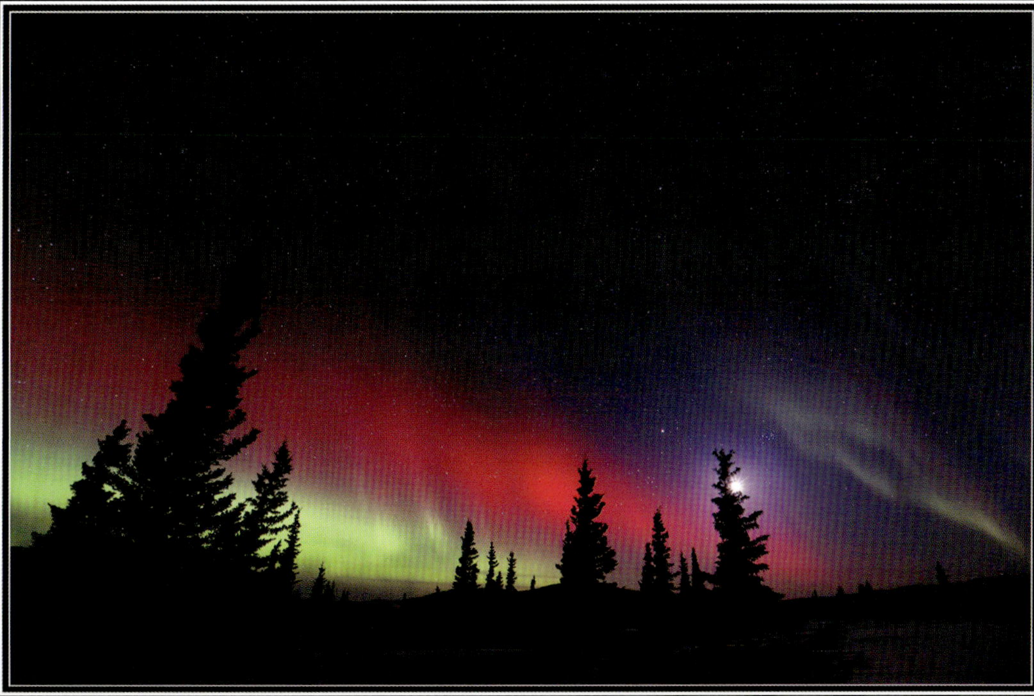

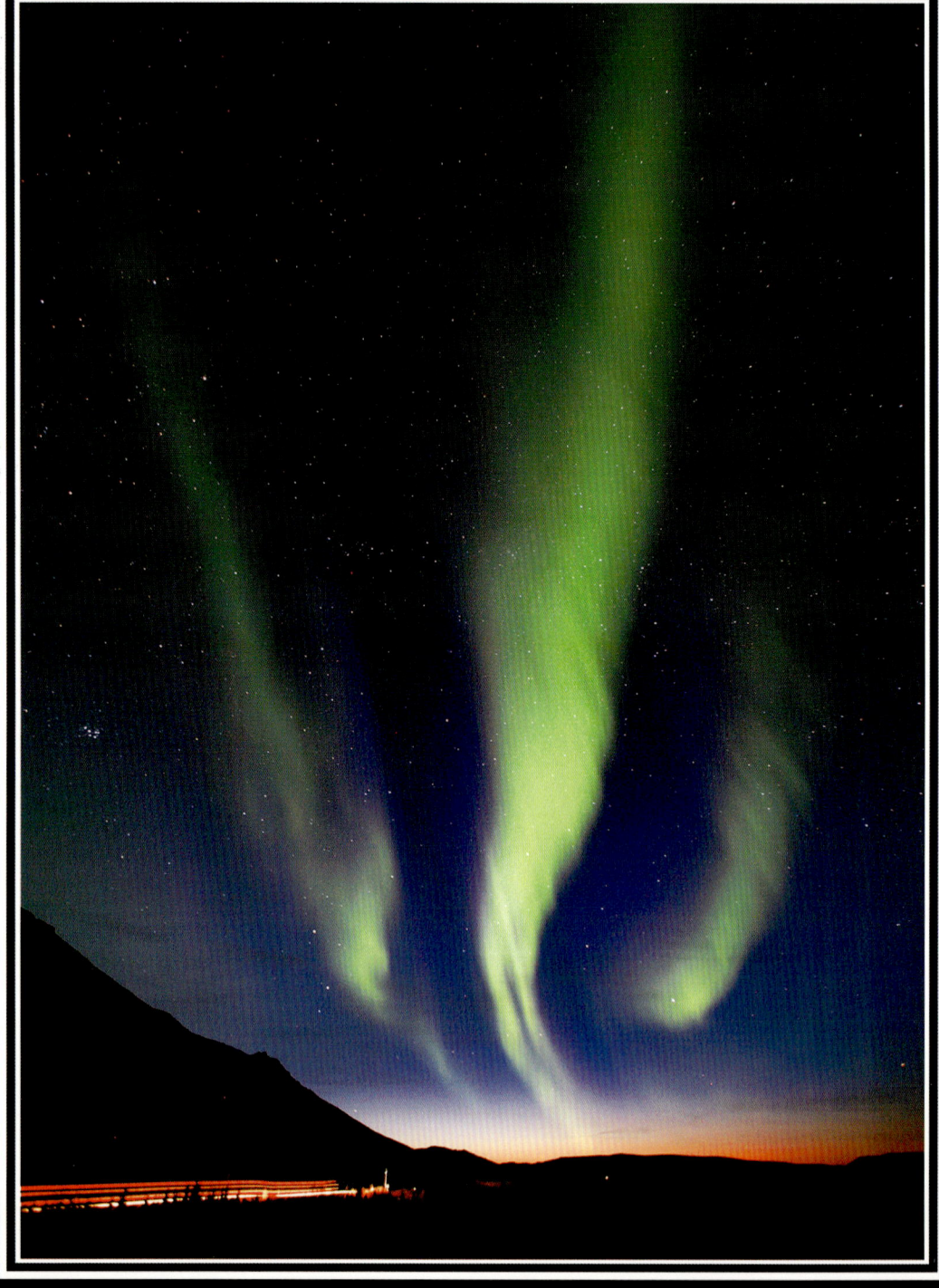

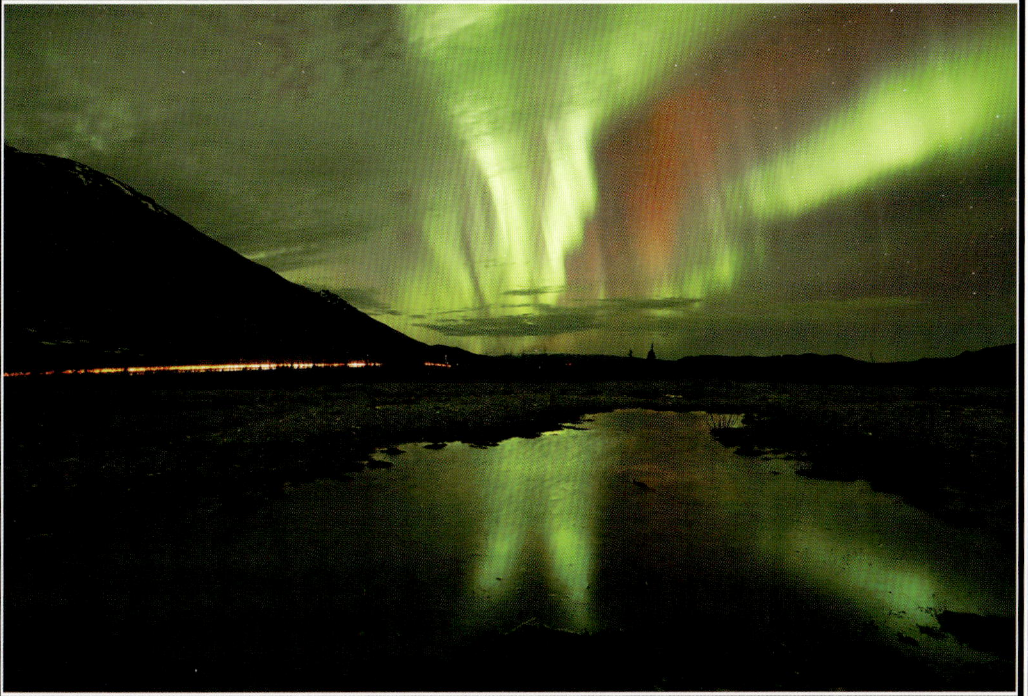

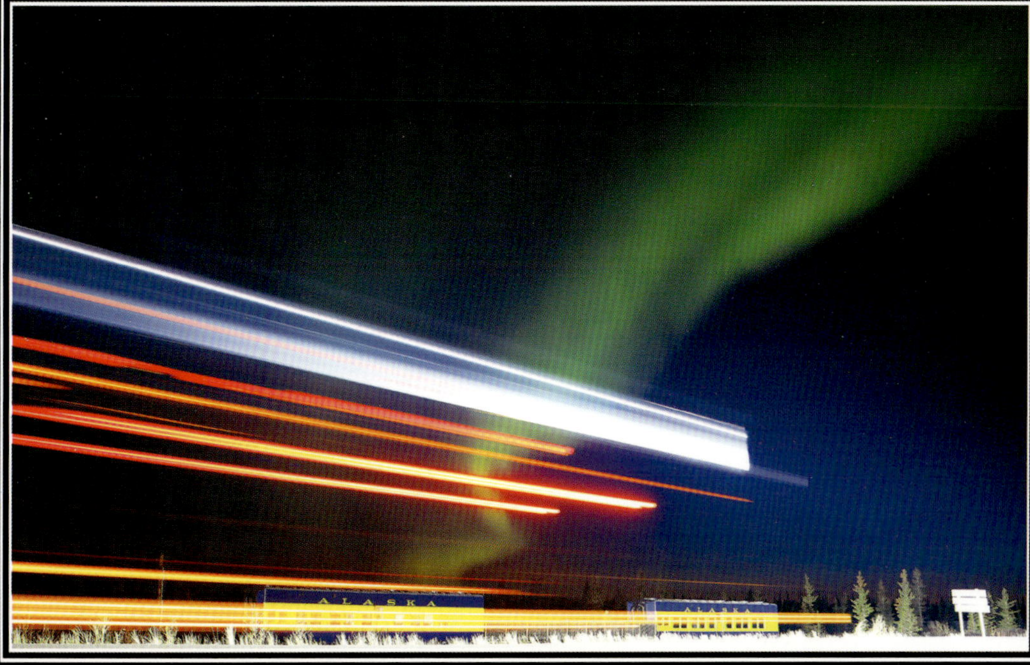

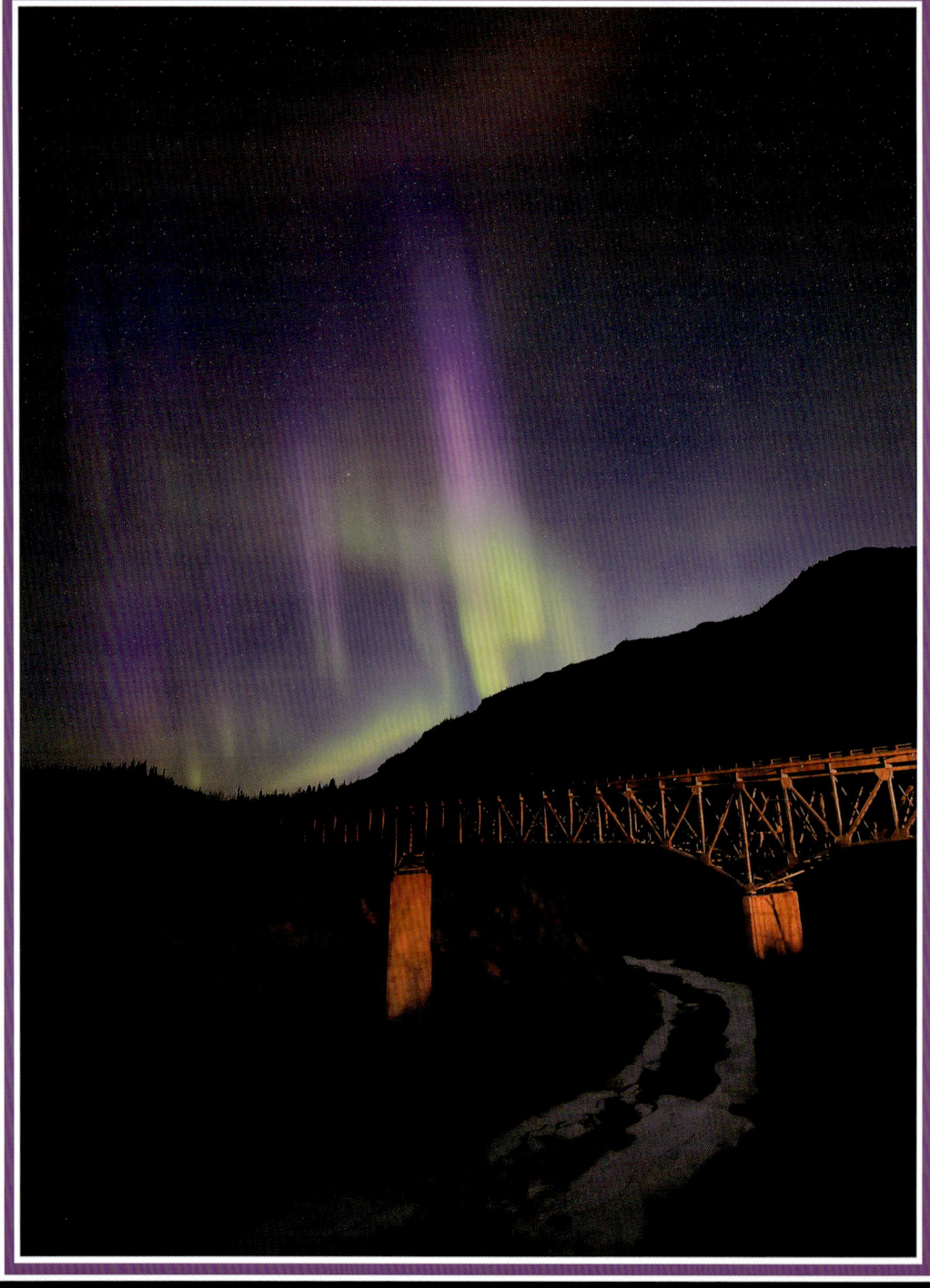

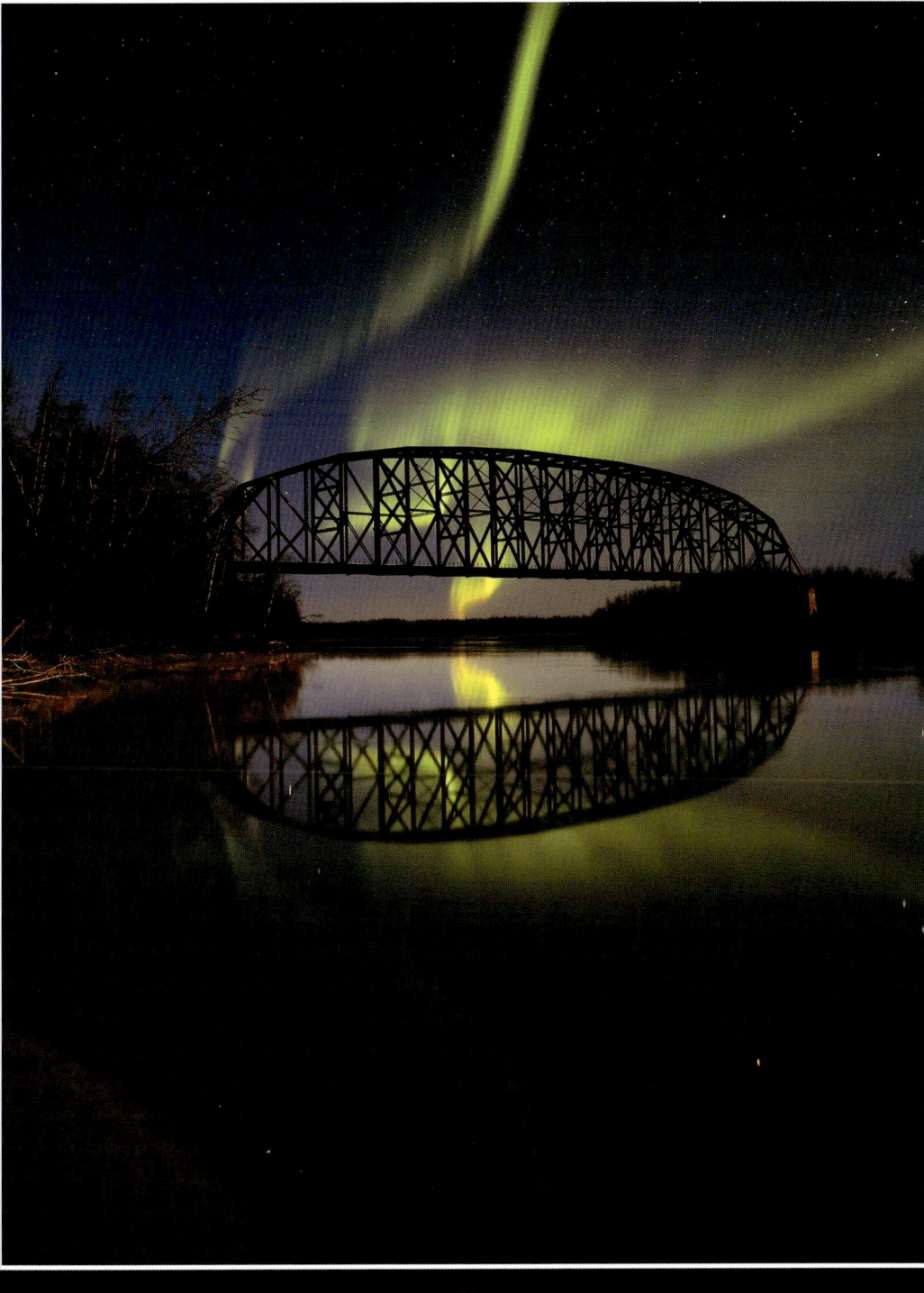

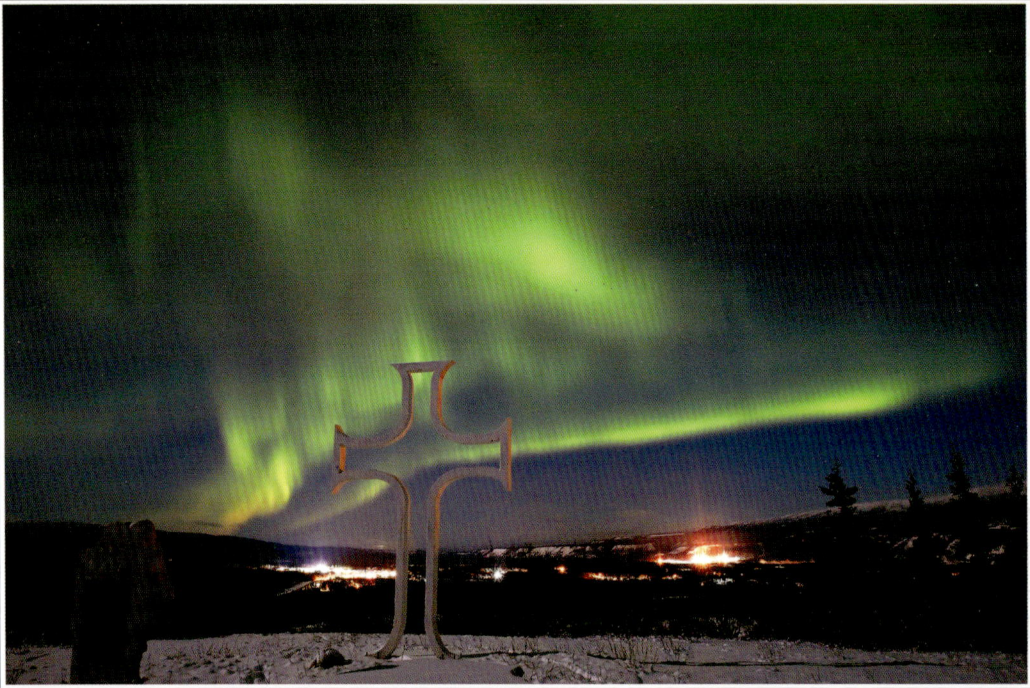

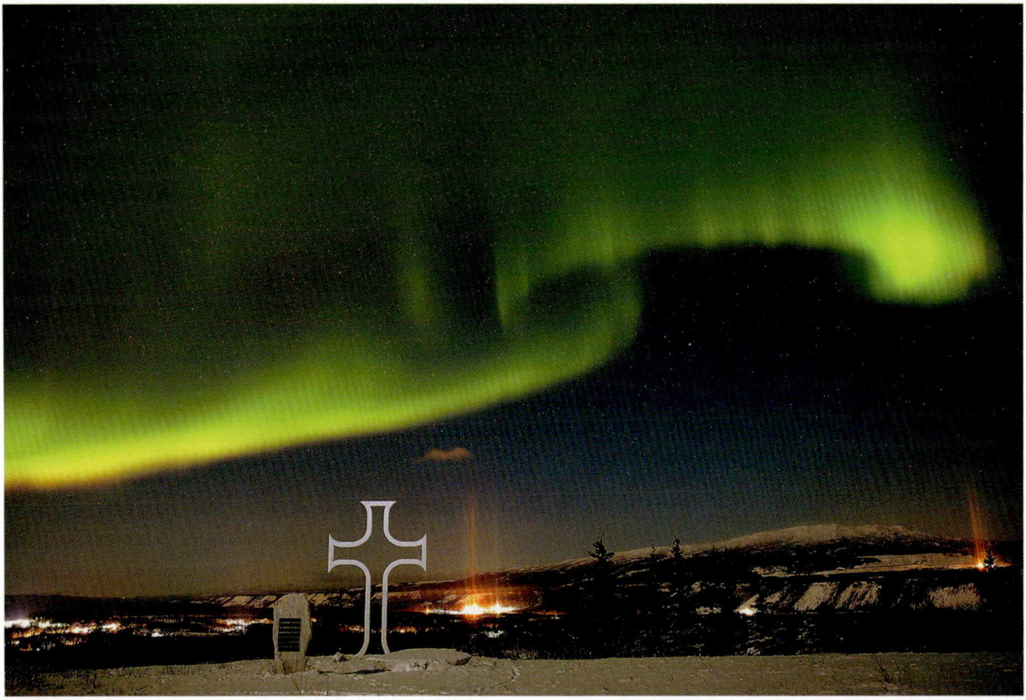

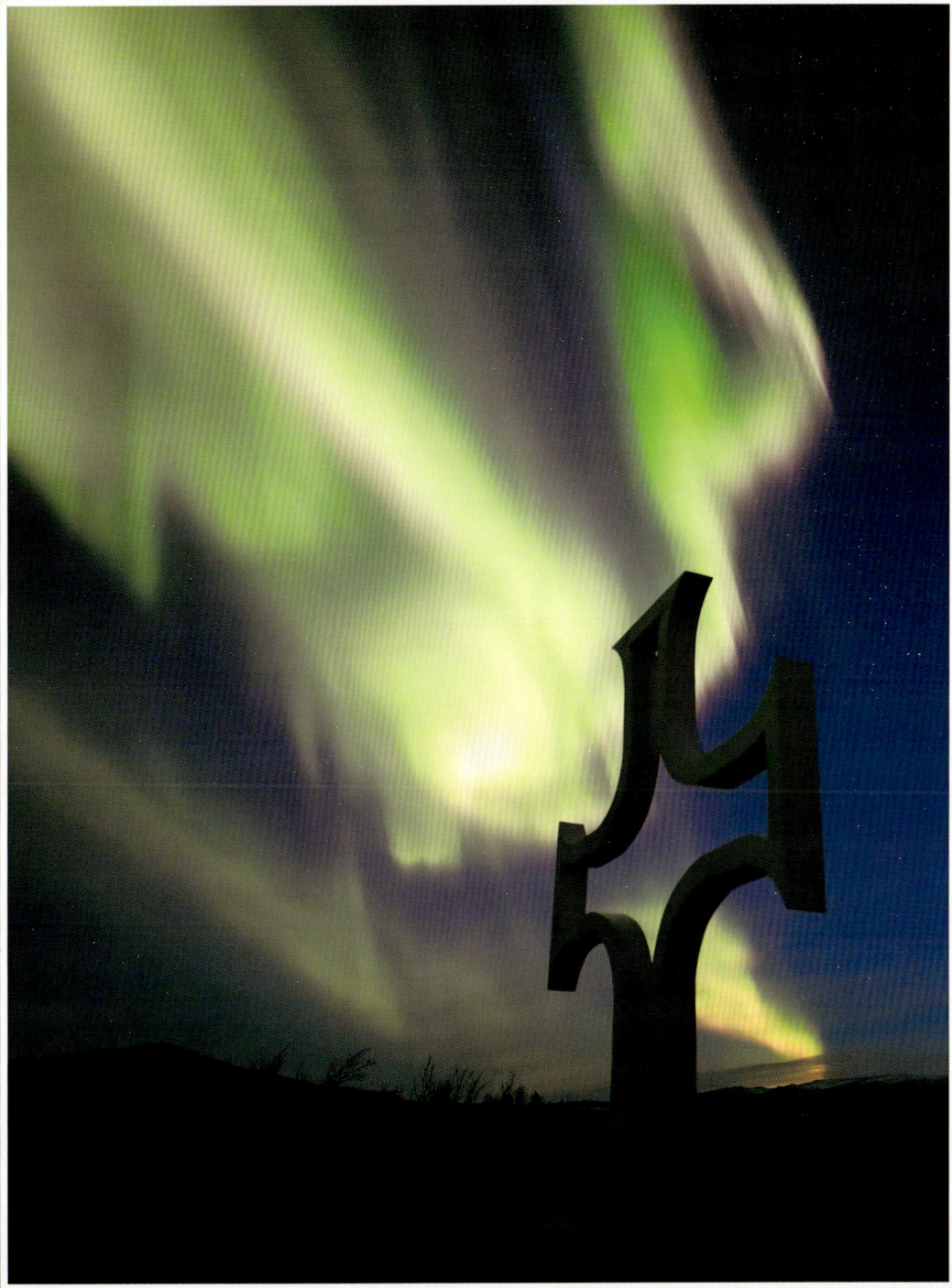

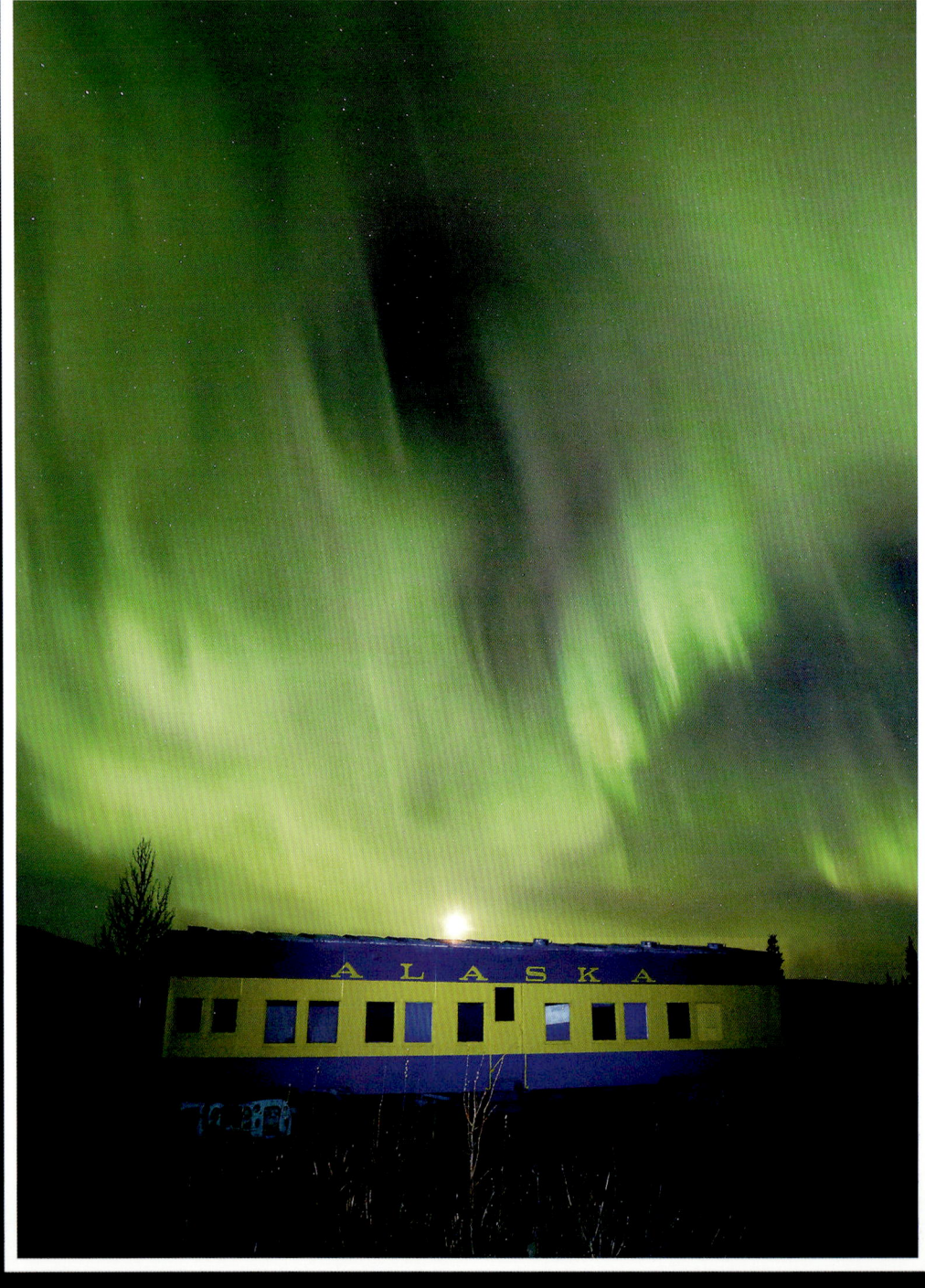

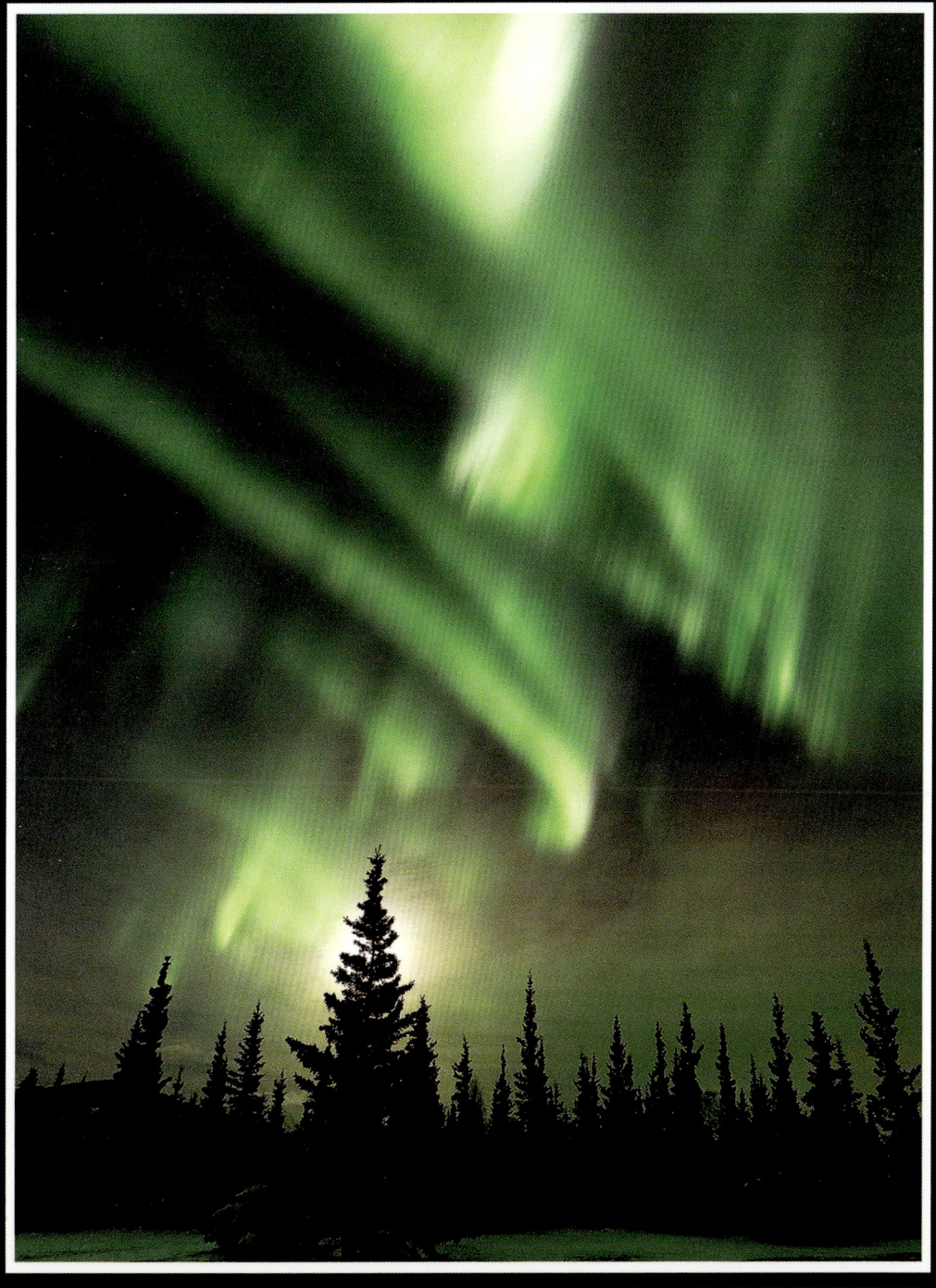

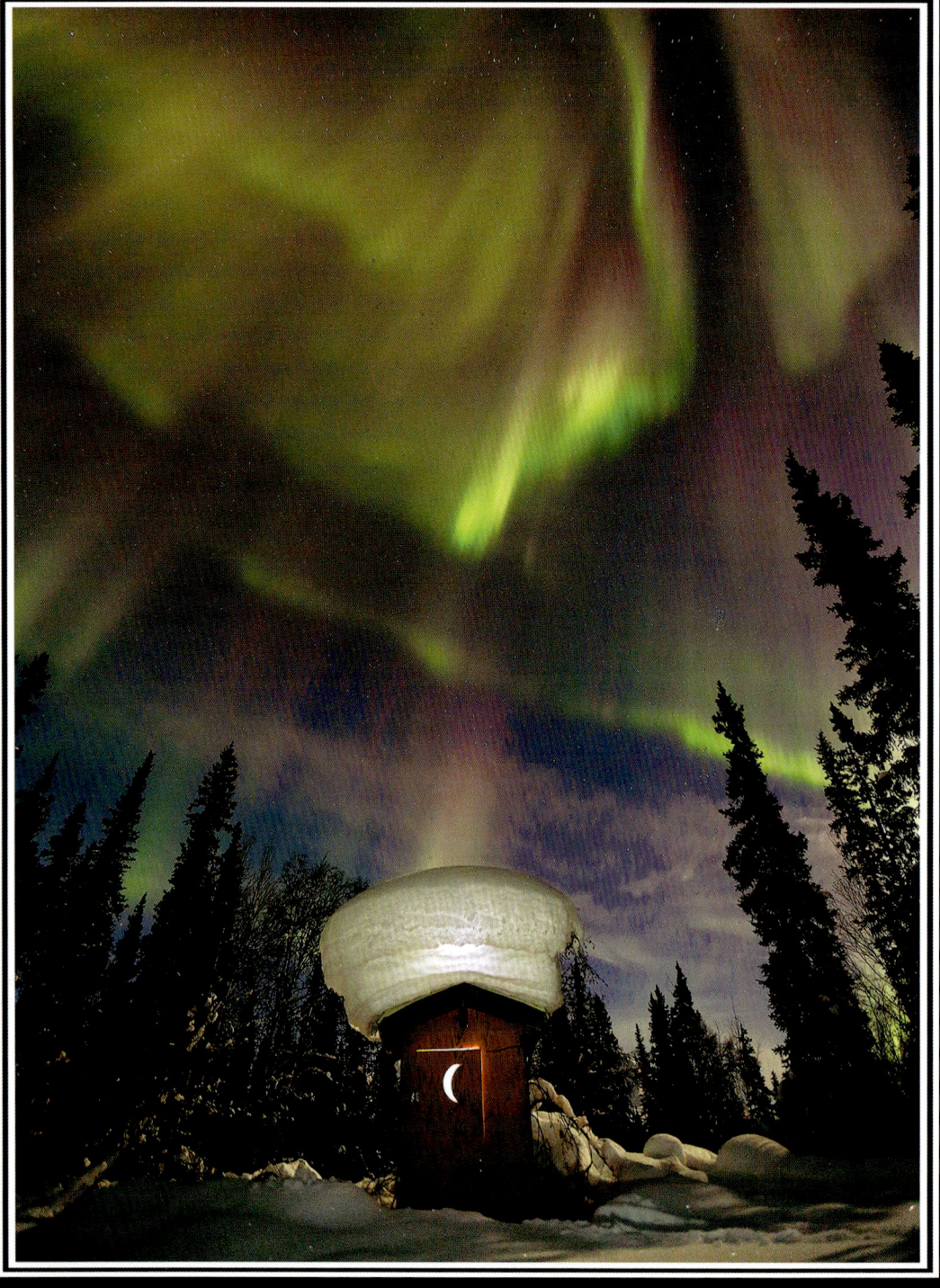

The Beauty of No Indoor Plumbing

I just went outside to pee
and much to my aglee,
it's thirty below
and the sky is aglow
with northern lights to see.

The northern lights, you see,
can help to set you free.
You'll stand and stare
with frozen nose hair
and forget you came out to pee.

If you give the lights a chance,
they'll put you in a trance,
from green to red,
as you lay back your head
and watch their magical dance.

It seems from the end of September
until I just can't remember,
it gets so darn cold
and the dark gets real old,
but the dance of the Lights keeps you limber.

You'll feel so warm inside
and the smile you just can't hide;
while watching the Lights
on cold winter nights,
you really can't beat the ride.

It's a ride so pure and free,
it's a ride you just have to see.
At thirty below
and the sky aglow,
don't forget you came out to pee.

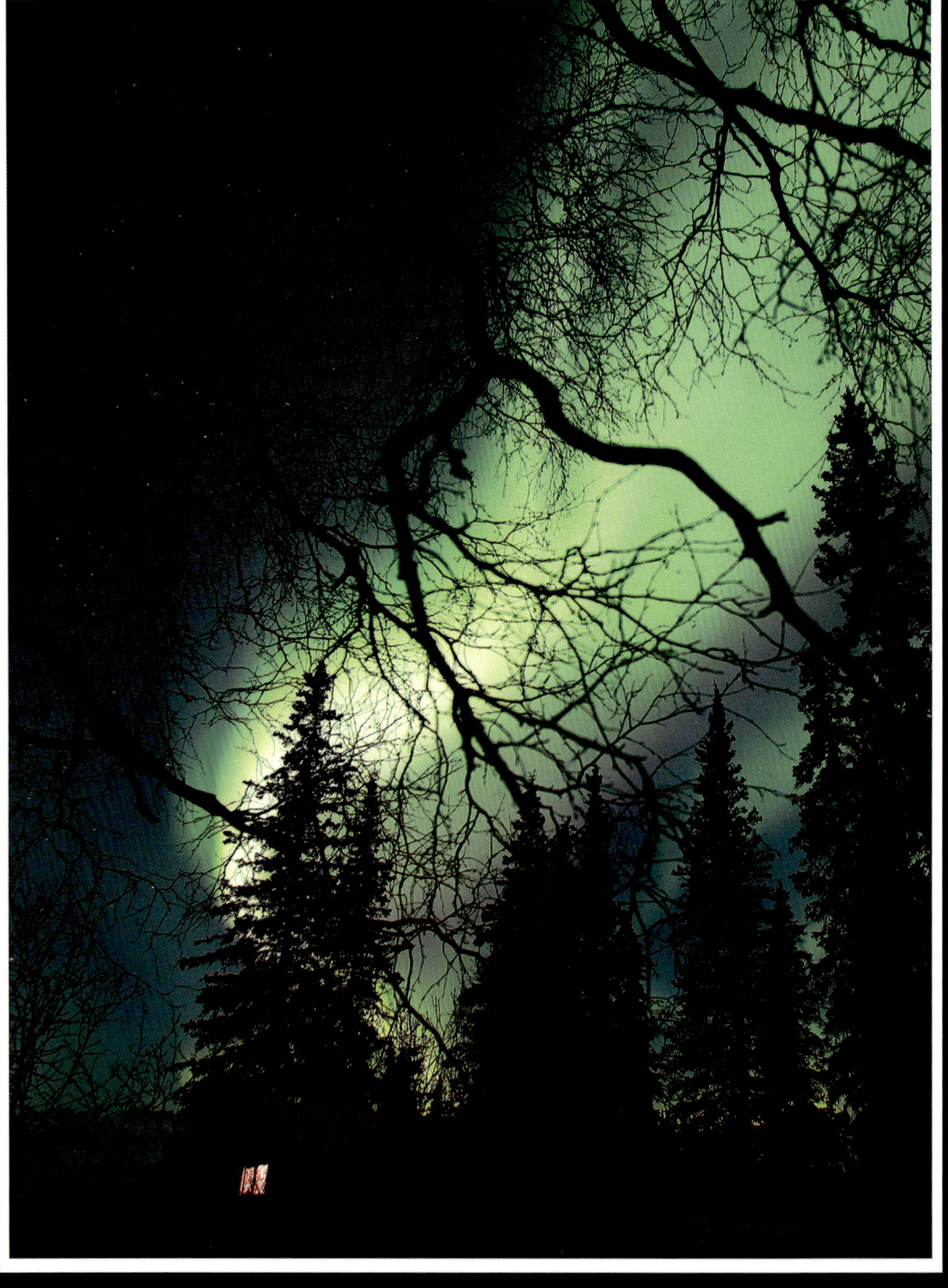

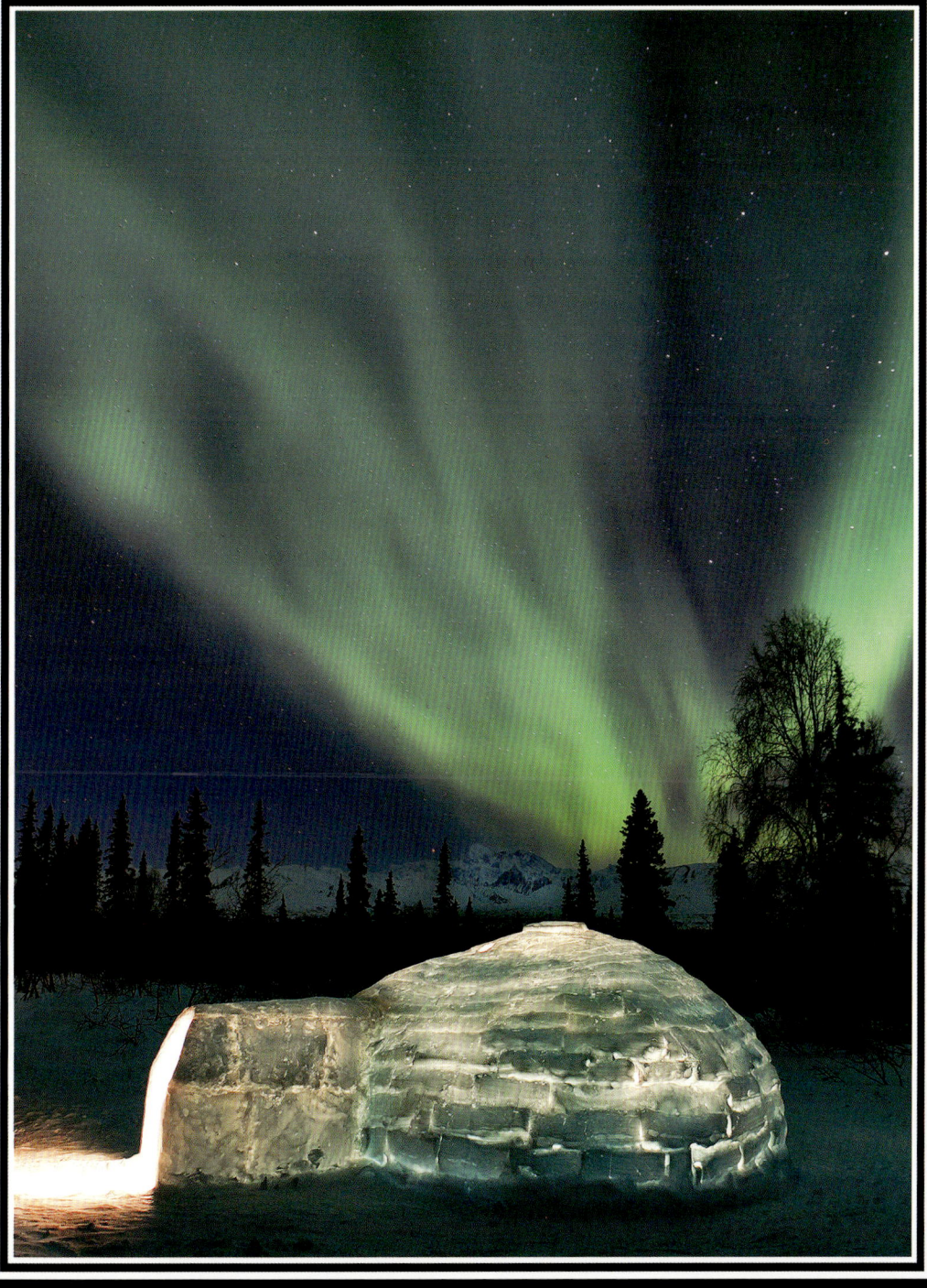

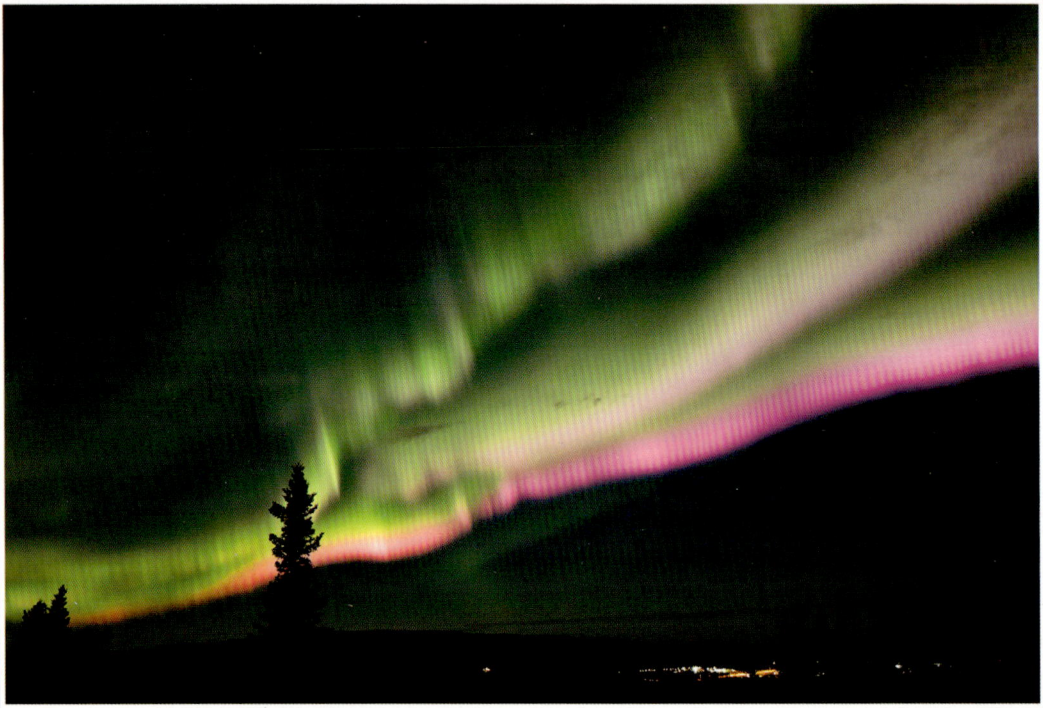

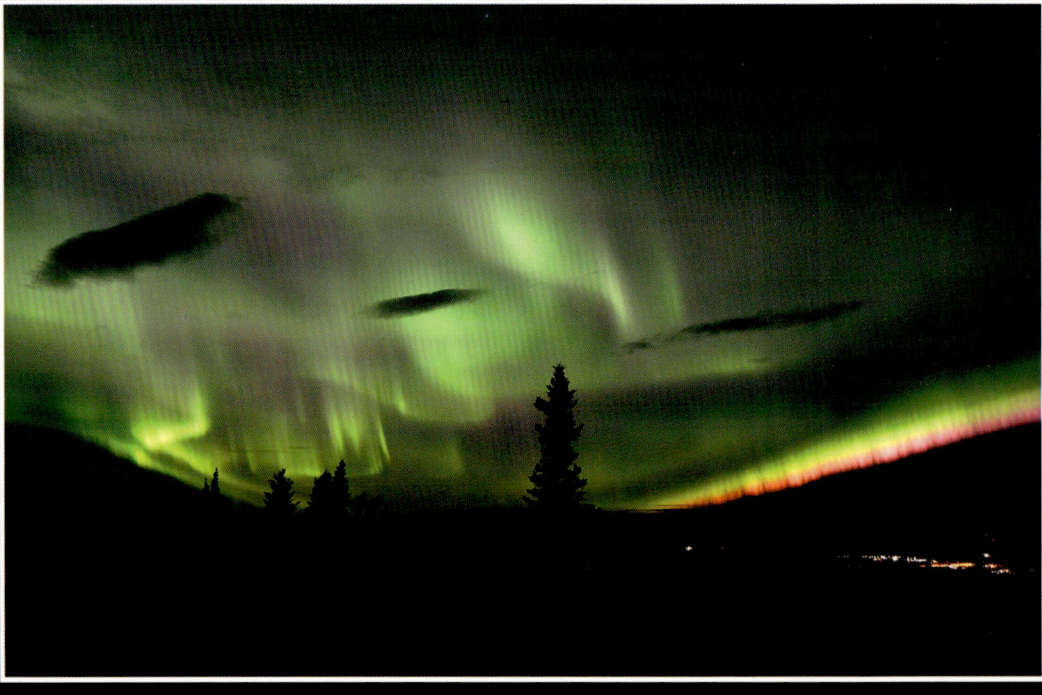

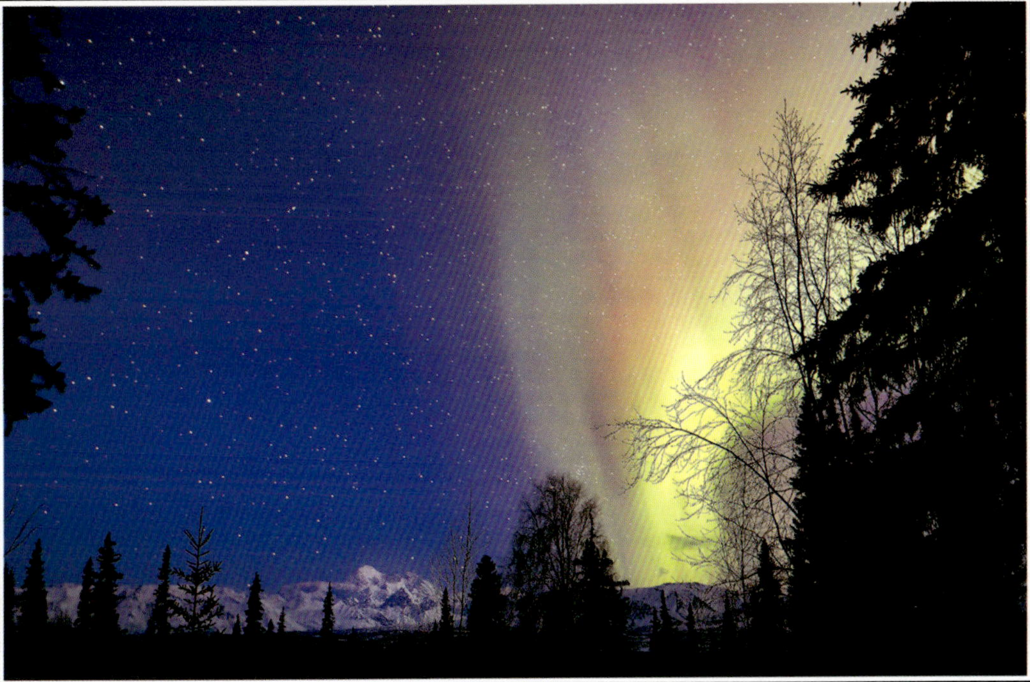

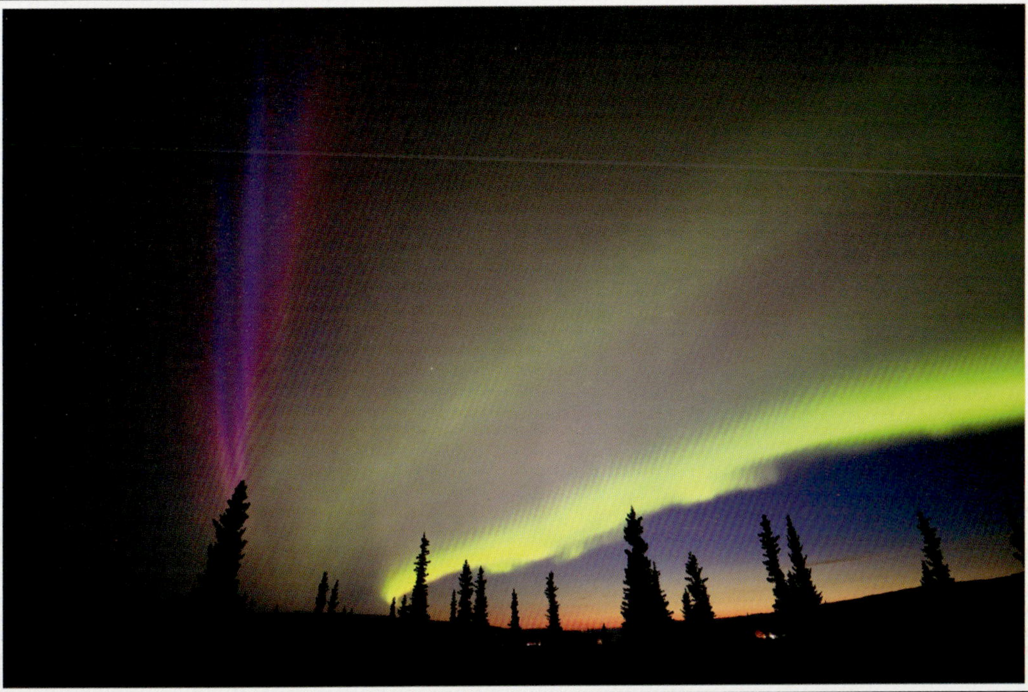

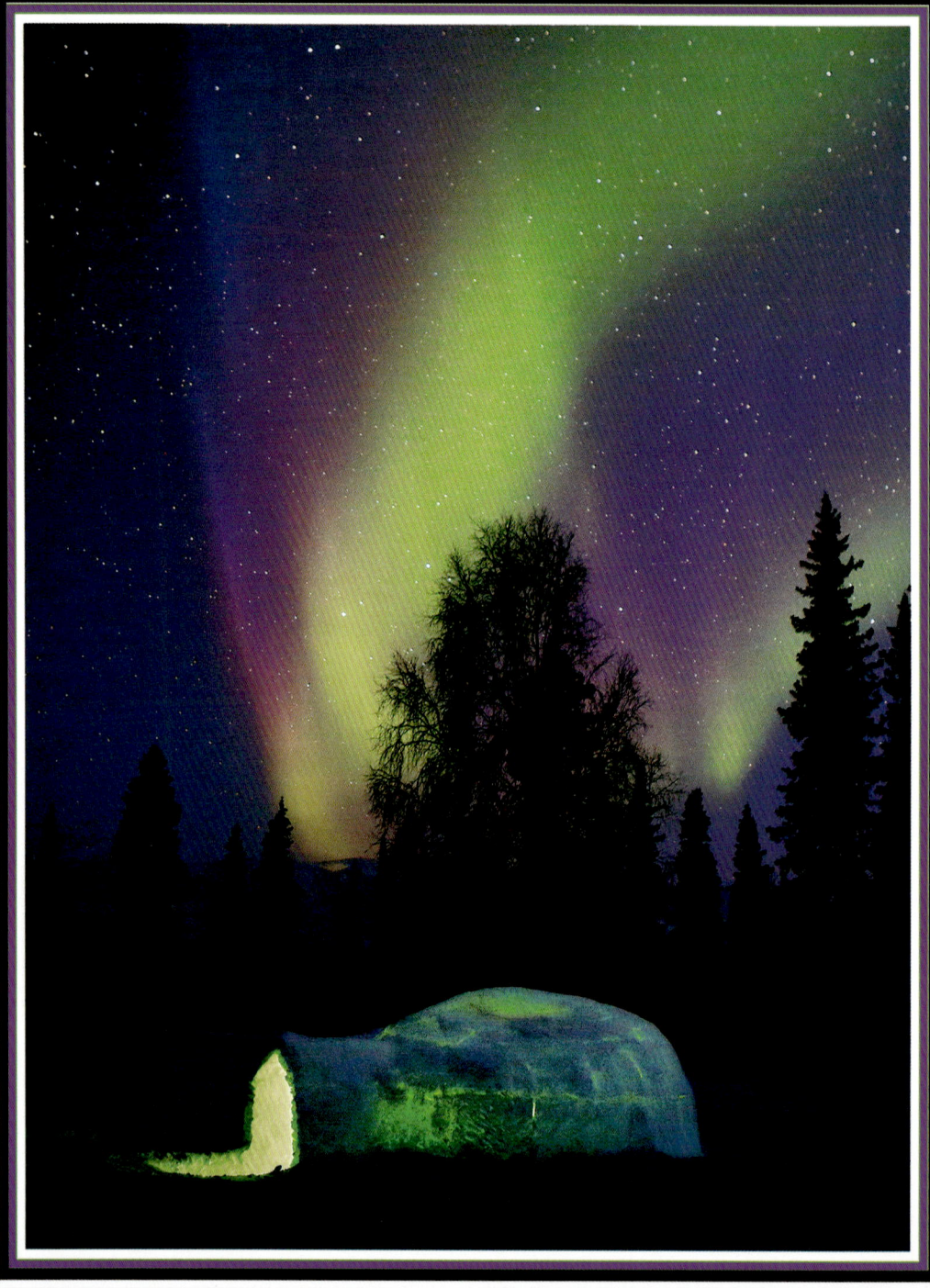

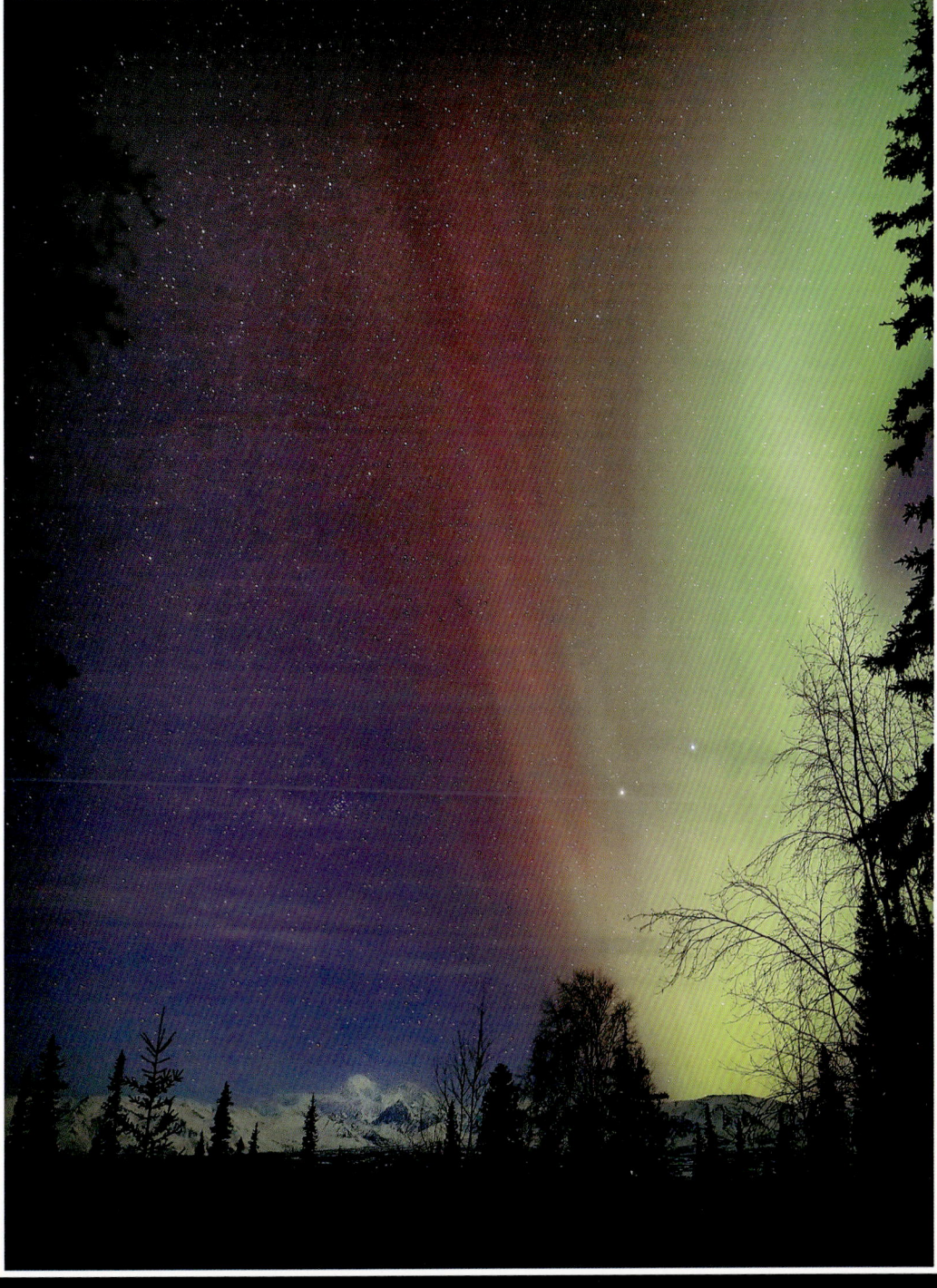

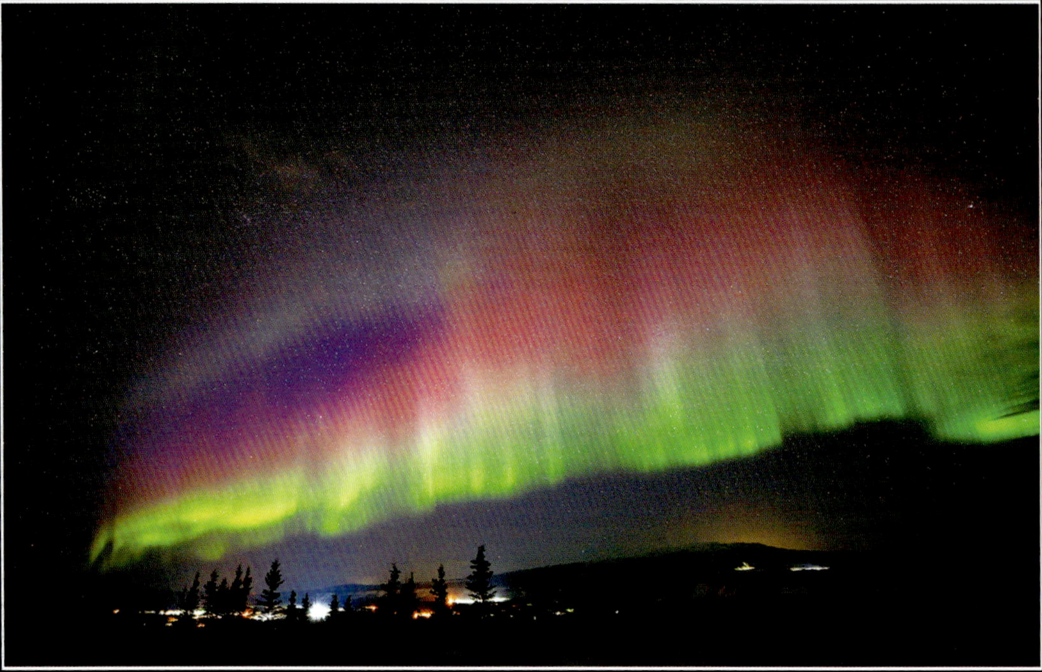

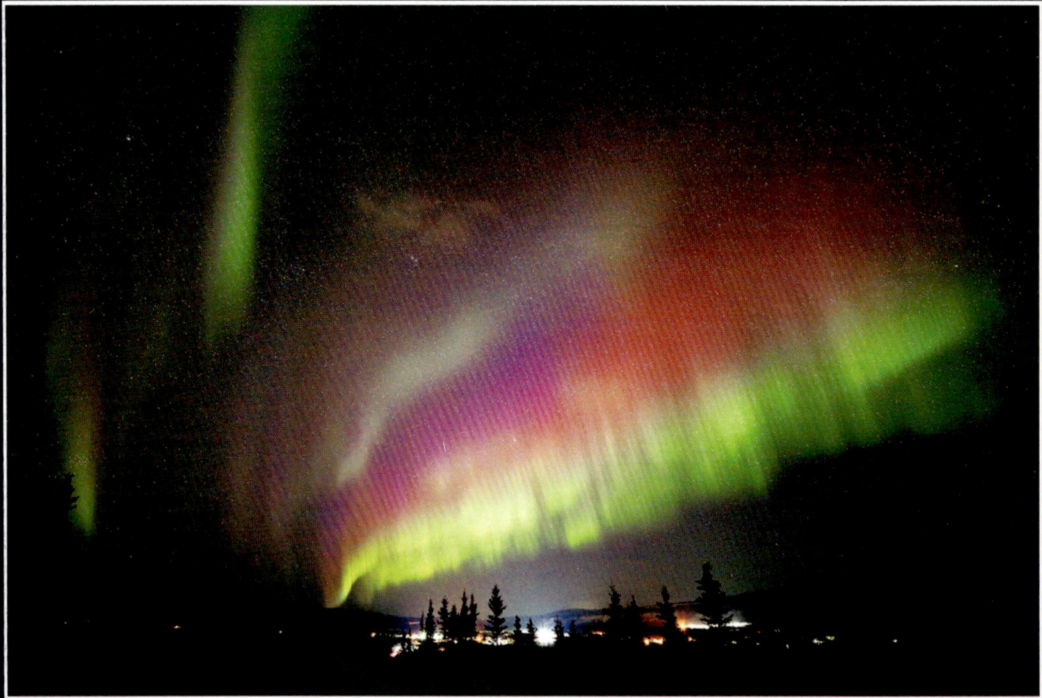

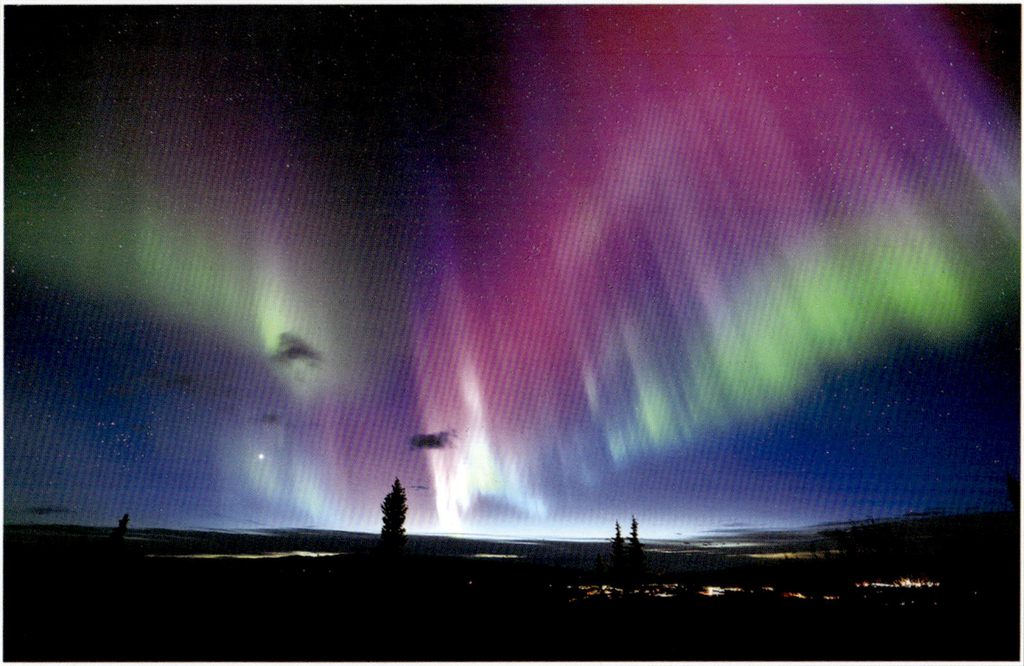

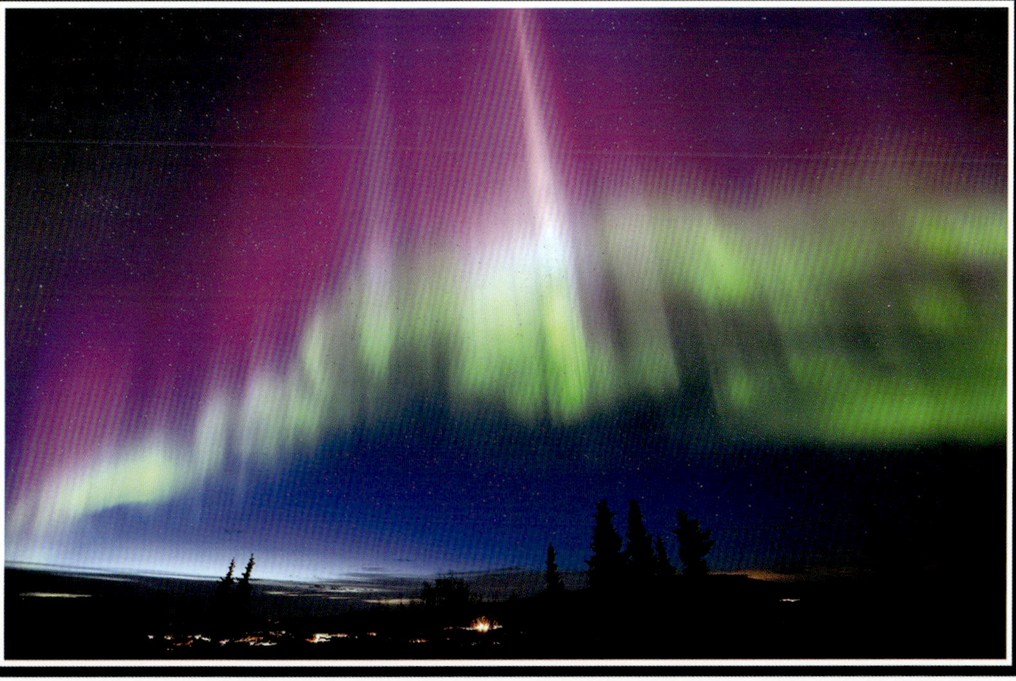

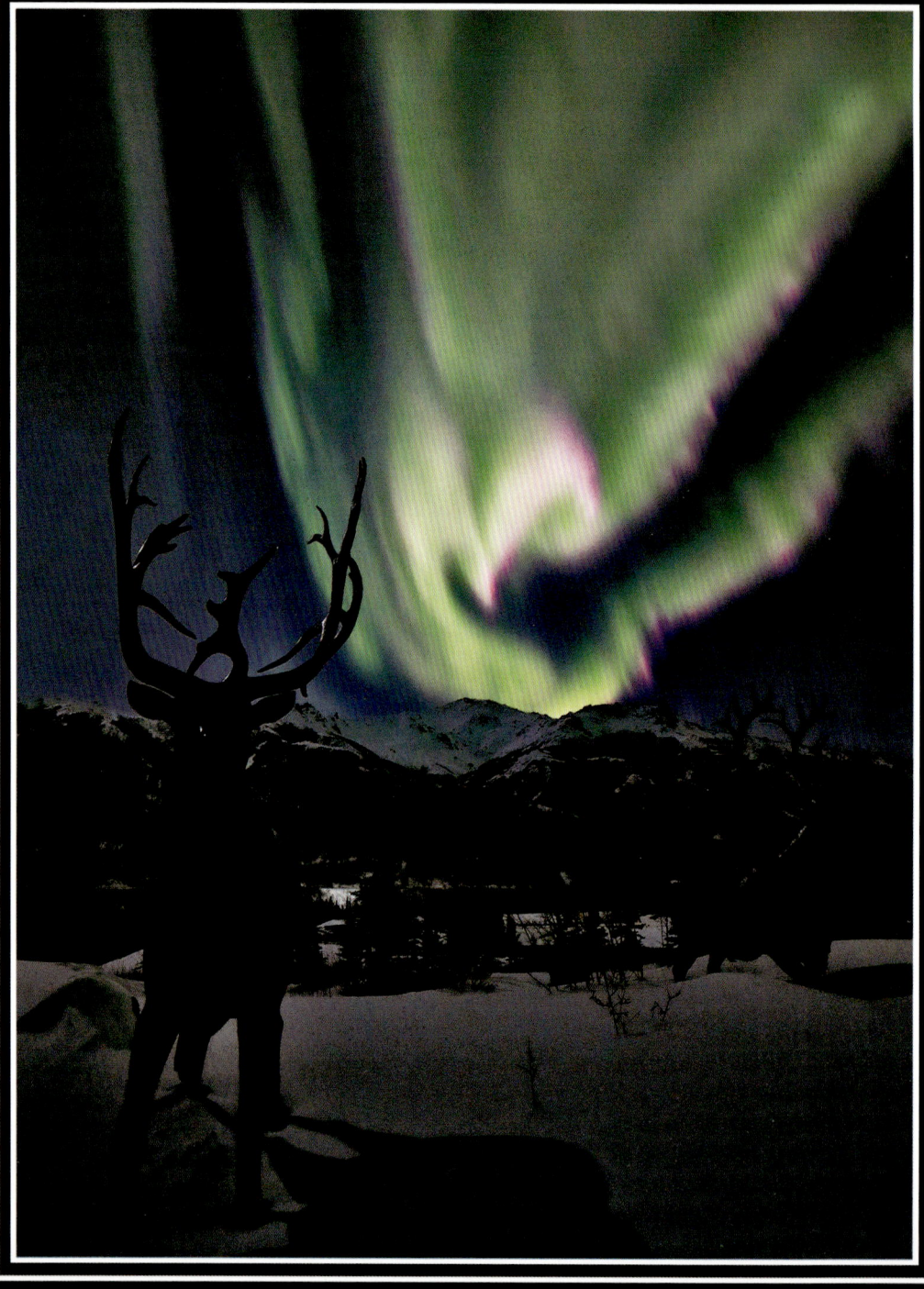

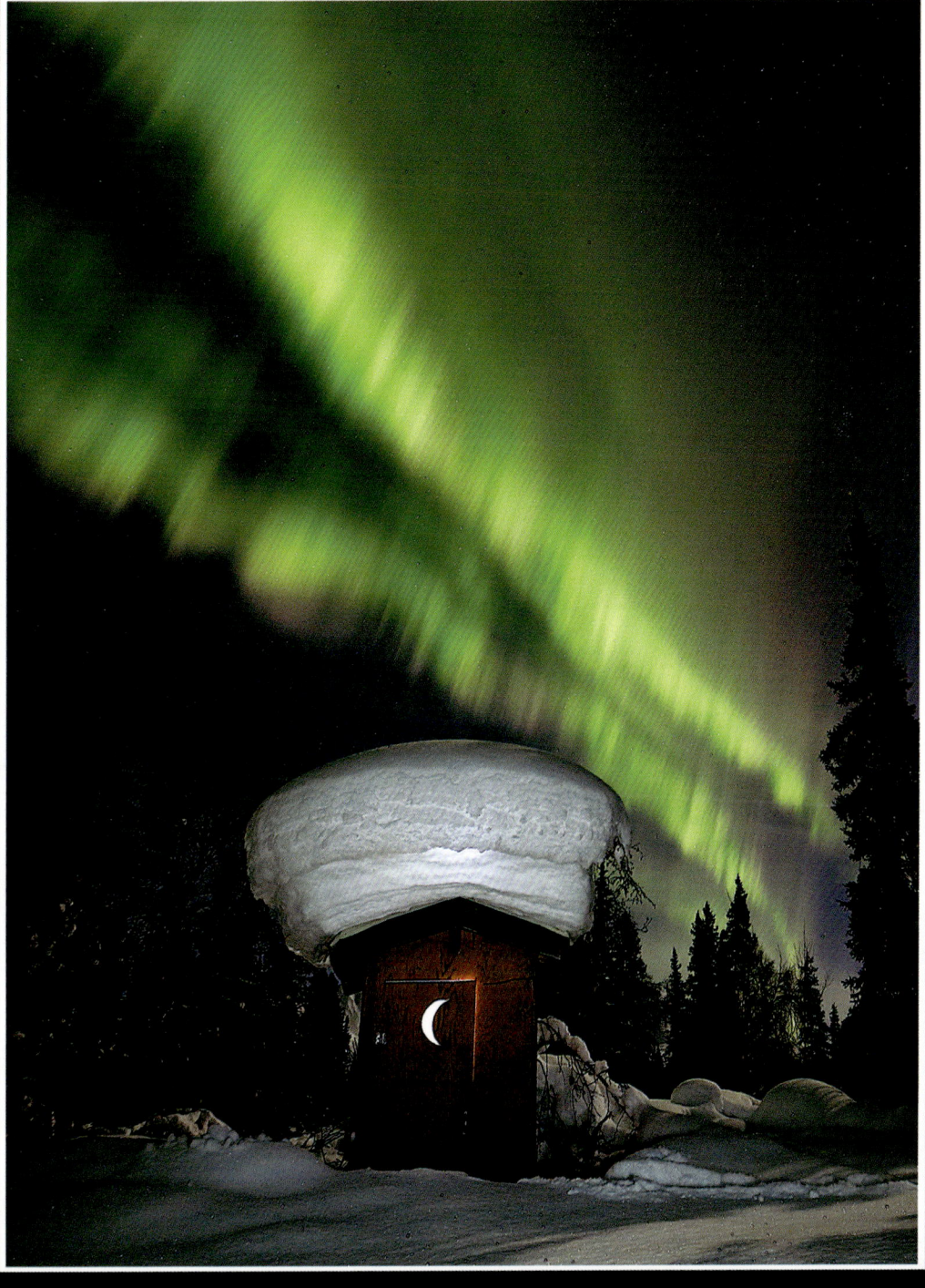

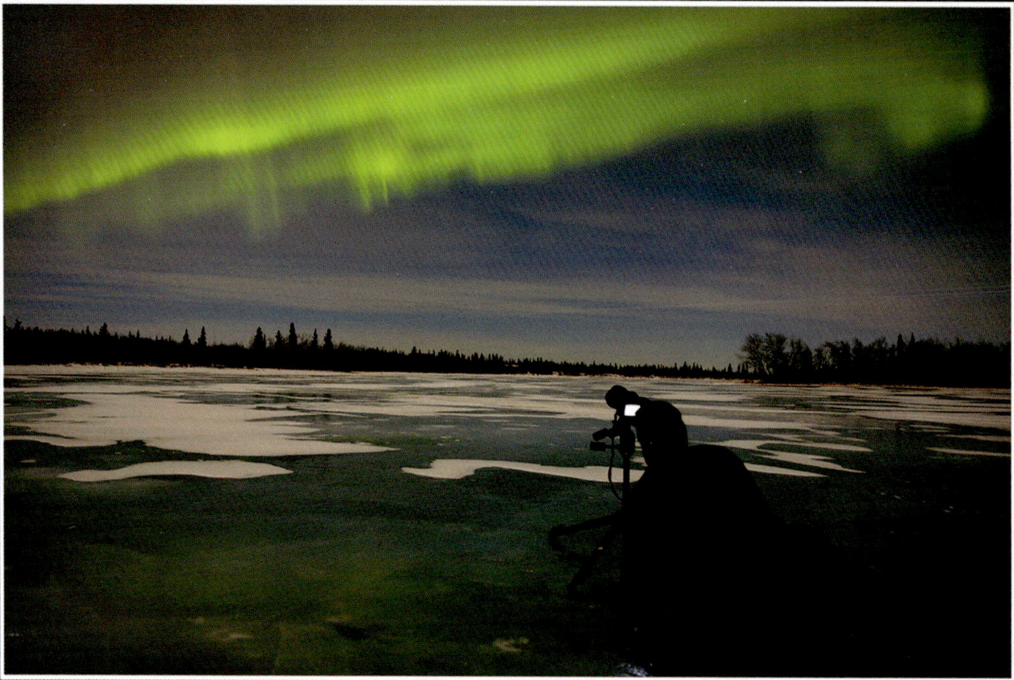

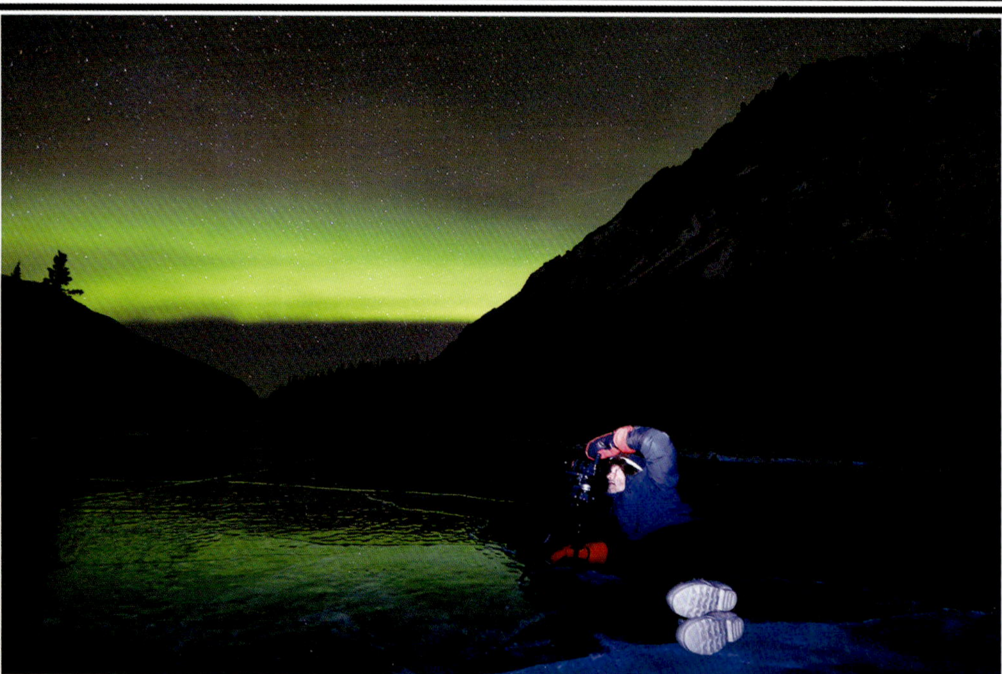

About the Photographer / Poet

Jimmy Tohill was born in 1959 in Dallas, Texas. He started taking pictures of wildlife and the great outdoors when he was 10 and began writing poetry about his passions when he was 13. Tohill attended Fort Lewis College in Durango, Colorado where he studied natural history, biology, skiing and mountain climbing. After falling in love with nature and adventure photography Jimmy started his first professional photography business in Durango in 1981 where he shot white water rafting photos on the Animas River, ski area photos at Purgatory ski area, weddings, portraits and wildlife and landscape images. In 1987 Tohill made a move north to Alaska to be a river guide and photographer at Denali National Park. He ended up guiding many places around Alaska and finally bought land in Healy, just 10 miles north of Denali Park, in 1994 and, with his lovely wife, Vicki, began building their scribe fit log home. They lived in a 12' x 16' cabin with no running water for 6 years while they hand built their home, out of pocket. They now live with the comforts of running water in their cozy log cabin in Healy. Jimmy and Vicki have owned and operated Old Sourdough Studio at the McKinley Chalet Resort in Denali since 1998. Old Sourdough Studio is a very unique photography studio with a state of the art digital lab that also specializes in taking white water rafting photos on the Nenana River.

The northern lights have truly fascinated Tohill since he first saw them while grooming ski runs in a snow cat at Purgatory Ski Area in southwest Colorado back in the mid 1980s. He has become quite passionate and very devoted to viewing and photographing the aurora borealis since 2006, spending entire nights out jogging in place to stay warm while waiting through the lulls of auroral storms. Living on the north side of the Alaska Range is a great place for viewing the aurora and Tohill has found a lot of interesting places to view and photograph them from. Tohill says, "Patience, awareness, devotion and acceptance come in handy in the pursuit of viewing and photographing the northern lights. Knowing how to operate and having the correct camera gear are huge factors for getting consistent, nice photographs. Knowing how to dress for and keep your camera gear operable in extremely low temperatures really helps as well. But most of all, it's best to just get outside and look up".

A sincere passion for life in Alaska continues to entice Tohill to get out and experience the wonderful Spirit of Alaska and capture it with his camera, his pen and his heart in an effort to, not only enhance his own life, but, attempt to share the magnificent splendors of the great outdoors with folks from all over the world.

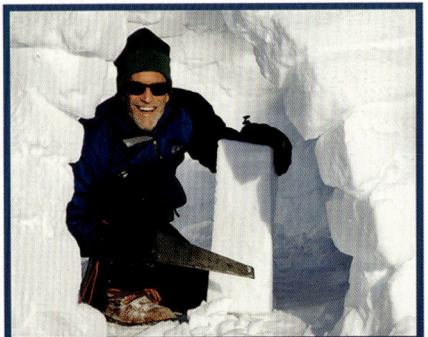

photo by Vicki Tohill

Index

1 ~ Opening page - Alaska Railroad trestle bridge over the Tanana River at Nenana
2 ~ Copyright page
3 ~ Table of Contents / Jimmy and Vicki Tohill in canoe on the frozen Otto Lake
4 ~ Classic igloo built by the Tohills at their Indian River remote cabin ~ April 14, 4 am
5 ~ Explanations and Observations
6 ~ Explanations and Observations (cont.)
7 ~ Rare, mostly pink aurora over Healy just after sunset ~ April 9, 11:25 pm
8 ~ Sunrise casts its glow to the north as the aurora lightly curtains above ~ April 19, 3:06 am
9 ~ An auroral swirl among the tall spruce with Alaska Range ~ Dec. 20, 8:36 pm
10 ~ Dancing lights on the north side of the Alaska Range and Denali National Park
11 ~ Poem: The Spirit of Alaska ~ Aurora Edition
12 ~ A colorful display at the Healy Cemetery with a near full moon ~ March 17, 12:16 am
13 ~ A very active display with an exploding corona straight overhead ~ Nov. 3, 12:41am
14 ~ Clouds rolling in during an active auroral storm over Healy ~ Sept. 27, 10:30ish pm
15 ~ With the coming clouds, this storm looks like a giant auroral tornado ~ Sept. 27, 10:34 pm
16 ~ Over the interior town of Healy just after sunset ~ April 9, 11:36 pm
17 ~ Igloo built by the Tohills with Denali in the distance and with Venus and Jupiter
18 ~ From near Chulitna Pass looking west at a full moon shining on Denali (20,310')
19 ~ Nice yellows appear during pre-sunrise over Denali (20,310') March 21, 6:08 am
20 ~ Looking out Tohill's north window with his feet on dresser and east window with icicles
21 ~ Poem: Dance of the Lights
22 ~ Poem: Dance of the Lights (cont.) / lights in the spruce ~ March 21, 5:42 am
23 ~ Tohill home nestled in the woods in Healy
24 ~ Spruce top full moon with a streak of lights ~ October 9, 12:12 am
25 ~ Swirling, curtaining displays over frozen Otto Lake with bright moon ~ March 1, 12ish am
26 ~ A rare, mostly red/purple display above the Tohill's home in Healy ~ Nov. 13, 7:21 pm
27 ~ A colorful show pulsating into coronas during a rising moon ~ Nov. 3, 12:53/1:41 am
28 ~ Lights, setting moon above Dry Creek drainage north of Denali N.P. ~ March 17, 12:24 am
29 ~ Poem: Cold and Dark
30 ~ Poem: Cold and Dark (cont.) / fast moving, brilliant display over Tohill's Healy yard
31 ~ Vivid curtains over interior town of Healy ~ March 17, right around midnight
32 ~ A cool, purple-blue aurora over the old Denali National Park sign ~ April 22, 3:23 am
33 ~ New Denali National Park sign 2017 (thanks Marianne Stolz, Bill Berry and Land Cole) ~ March 23, 4:25 am
34 ~ Under the Mountain Studio and Kantishna Air at Skyline Lodge, Kantishna ~ Sept. 15, 2 am
35 ~ Aurora streaking above solar panels at Skyline Lodge, Moose Creek valley, Kantishna
36 ~ Screaming fast aurora over frozen Otto Lake, north side of Alaska Range ~ March 18, 2:20 am
37 ~ Denali Chamber of Commerce and historical Mtn. View Grocery in Healy ~ April 20, 1 am
38 ~ Looking up the driveway of Denali Dome Home, Healy / aurora just south of Healy

Index

39 ~ World famous Denali Dome Home B & B in Healy ~ April 22, 1:01 am
40 ~ Christmas lights illuminate spruce trees at the Tohill's in Healy with a mild aurora in the sky
41 ~ Tohill's Christmas star with a colorful auroral display, Healy ~ Dec. 19, 8:52 pm
42 ~ A crack in the ice of this lake near Cantwell accentuates the auroral band ~ March 15, 11 pm
43 ~ Poem: An Awakening of Light / self portrait on frozen Otto Lake ~ March 3, 3:16 am
44 ~ The moon and vivid aurora reflect off of the snow free ice of Otto Lake ~ March 29, 3:38 am
45 ~ Warm winds made the ice of Otto Lake snow free revealing this view ~ March 1, 2 am
46 ~ Warm winds made the ice of Otto Lake snow free revealing this view ~ March 18, 2:30 am
47 ~ Self portrait in a canoe on the frozen Otto Lake with the sky ablaze ~ March 3, 4:06 am
48 ~ A faint aurora pulsates into an explosion over Mt. Healy, Denali N.P. ~ March 18, 12:38 am
49 ~ After freeze up, warm winds made the ice of Otto Lake snow free revealing this splendid view
50 ~ The north end of Wonder Lake in Denali National Park reflects a very tranquil aurora
51 ~ A full moon along with the aurora light up the sky over the Tanana River at Nenana looking downstream at the Parks Hwy double trestle bridge ~ Oct.14, 2:03 am
52 ~ A few clouds in the right location along with some jamming aurora can give the night sky a very unique look, over Healy ~ Sept. 27, 10:30ish pm
53 ~ Poem: Precious Moments / rare, mostly pink aurora just after sunset, Healy ~ April 9, 11:25 pm
54 ~ A few clouds in the right location along with some jamming aurora can give the night sky a very ethereal feel, over Dry Creek ~ March 27, 2 am
55 ~ A few clouds in the right location along with some jamming aurora can give the night sky a pretty cool look, over Healy Creek / over Dry Creek ~ March 27, 1 - 2 am
56 ~ Orange-pink aurora above orange glow from sunset/sunrise to the north over Healy ~ April 23, 1:04 am / purple and green curtains race across the sky around 1 am on March 27 / swirling aurora over Healy just before sunrise ~ April 20, 2:00 am
57 ~ A lone purple shaft of light rising up from paradise ~ April 19, 1:53 am
58 ~ A rapidly pulsating corona straight overhead, Indian River cabin ~ Dec. 20, 7:45 pm
59 ~ One minute earlier than pg. 58 and looking toward the Talkeetna Mtns lit up by the moon
60 ~ An intense auroral storm culminating in overhead exploding coronas of color - sequence shots taken a minute apart ~ Nov. 3, looking west at 1:41 am and straight up at 1:42 am
61 ~ Poem: Colors Swirling in the Sky
62 ~ Poem: Colors Swirling in the Sky (cont.) / a breathtaking auroral corona ~ Nov. 3, 12:42 am
63 ~ Can you see a ghost in this corona ? / how about a dog (Underdog) in this corona?
64 ~ Colors streaking through the sky, north of Denali N.P. ~ Nov. 3, 1:38 am
65 ~ The aurora curtains above a setting moon on the north side of the Alaska Range ~ March 17, 1:52 am
66 ~ From atop Chulitna Butte under a full moon - top, looking northeast at Talkeetna Mtns and , bottom, west at Denali and the Alaska Range ~ March 11, around midnight
67 ~ Rainbow aurora over Mt. Sugarloaf / sunset aurora over Nenana Valley

Index

68 ~ Alaska RR train lights up the Nenana gorge below Mt. Sugarloaf with aurora streaking above / pond starting to freeze up with moon and mild aurora ~ April 13, 1:20ish am
69 ~ Tohill driveway in Healy ~ Dec. 8, 10:58 pm / pond starting to freeze up ~ April 13, 1:23 am
70 ~ Purple Rays all in the sky; rare, purple-blue display, Denali N.P. ~ April 22, 3:19 am
71 ~ An intense red/green display looking to the south over Mt. Healy ~ March 17, 12:51 am
72 ~ Swirling streaks at sunset over truck on Parks Hwy, Antler Creek ~ March 25, 10:42 pm
73 ~ Freight trucks heading north to Fairbanks on the Parks Hwy just north of Denali N.P.
74 ~ Windy Bridge on the Parks Hwy over the Nenana River gorge ~ April 22, 2:03 am
75 ~ Alaska RR trestle over the Tanana River at Nenana before freeze up ~ Oct. 14, 2:10 am
76 ~ Cross at the Healy Cemetery looking over the interior town of Healy at 31 below - notice the ice crystals in the air being lit up by the bright lights at Usibelli Coal Mine ~ Feb. 8, 12:40 am
77 ~ Cross at the Healy Cemetery with the aurora shining bright ~ April 23, 2:18 am
78 ~ Glowing sky as the moon sets over Alaska RR car at the Denali Park Hotel south of Healy
79 ~ The moon rises behind a white spruce as the aurora dances overhead ~ Nov. 3, 1:43 am
80 ~ An early evening storm during a full moon, Tohill's remote cabin outhouse ~ Dec 20, 8 pm
81 ~ Poem: The Beauty of No Indoor Plumbing
82 ~ Looking through birch branches at Tohill's remote cabin, Indian River ~ March 10, 1:39 am
83 ~ Denali sits high on the horizon above an igloo built by the Tohills at their remote cabin property, a lantern is inside the igloo illuminating it from within ~ March 16, 2:23 am
84 ~ A vivid, somewhat rare, orange turning to pink at the bottom of the aurora ~ Sept 27, 10 pm
85 ~ Denali (20,310') is lit up by the aurora and a rising sun, north of Denali State Park ~ March 21, 5:49 am / a rogue purple streak shoots up from a display following sunset over the interior town of Healy ~ April 19, 1:54 am
86 ~ Headlamp inside green water bottle lighting up igloo built by Tohills ~ April 14, 3:44 am
87 ~ Denali (20,310') stands high above the surrounding peaks of the Alaska Range ~ March 21, 4:39 am
88 ~ Quick sequence photos of a screaming, vivid display over Healy ~ March 27, 12:36 am
89 ~ Photos 35 seconds apart of a colorful, wildly curtaining aurora, Healy ~ April 9, 11:30 pm
90 ~ A fast moving, brilliant aurora along with a quarter moon light up Mt. Healy and silhouette two bronze caribou sculptures at the Denali Princess Wilderness Lodge in the Nenana Canyon at Denali ~ March 25, 1:14 am
91 ~ With a quick flash of a head lamp and a head lamp on inside, Tohill lit up the snow covered outhouse at he and his wife's remote cabin just north of Denali State Park between the Talkeetna Mtns. and the Alaska Range during a full moon ~ Dec. 20, 7:52 pm
92 ~ Self portraits on frozen Otto Lake (top) / on un-named lake, Cantwell (bottom)
93 ~ About the Photographer / Poet
94 ~ Index
95 ~ Index
96 ~ Index